# HEALING the
# WHOLE PERSON

## APPLICATIONS OF YOGA PSYCHOTHERAPY

Swami Ajaya

HIMALAYAN
INSTITUTE®
PRESS

Himalayan Institute Press
952 Bethany Turnpike
Honesdale, Pennsylvania 18431 USA

www.HimalayanInstitute.org

Printed in the United States of America

The paper used in this publication meets the minimum require-
ments of American National Standard for Information Sciences—
Permanence of Paper for Printed Library Materials, ANSI Z39.48-
1984.

© Images.com/Corbis-Medical Mantra

Library of Congress Cataloging-in-Publication Data

Ajaya, Swami, 1940-
  Healing the whole person : applications of yoga psychotherapy /
by Swami Ajaya.
      p. cm.
  Includes bibliographical references and index.
  ISBN 978-0-89389-275-3 (pbk. : alk. paper)
  1. Yoga--Therapeutic use. 2. Meditation--Therapeutic use. I.
Title.
  RC489.M43A43 2008
  616.89'1653--dc22
                                      2008009395

# HEALING the WHOLE PERSON

## APPLICATIONS OF YOGA PSYCHOTHERAPY

# CONTENTS

# INTRODUCTION

Michael P. Butler, PhD

YOGA IS MORE POPULAR THAN EVER with the
American public. Tens of millions practice some form of yoga
on a regular basis, and yoga-related products, such as books,
videos, and yoga mats, can be found in stores everywhere. It
has become so mainstream, in fact, that yoga has even been
used in advertising to sell a wide variety of other types of products to the general population, from health insurance to
automobiles to fast food.

It has become increasingly popular with both medical and
mental health professionals, as well, and has been the subject
of much empirical research. The practice of asana, for example, has been shown to increase relaxation and to improve
mood: it is associated with better mental health. Meditation,
one of yoga's most important practices, has been found to be
effective in the treatment of a wide variety of physical and psychological problems, including coronary artery disease, chronic
pain, anxiety, depression, and even several skin disorders.

Elements of yogic spirituality have also been incorporated
into several scientifically supported Western psychotherapies.
Marsha Linehan's Dialectical Behavior Therapy (DBT) and
the Acceptance and Commitment Therapy (ACT) of Steven
Hayes and colleagues, for example, both make use of con-

structs that are nearly identical to the yogic construct of *vairagya*, an attitudinal state characterized by simultaneous non-attraction and non-aversion. ACT also formally incorporates meditation into its efforts at teaching clients to be non-resistant toward their own undesirable but unavoidable internal and external experiences (tension resulting from resistance to experiences that cannot or should not be avoided has been shown to greatly intensify our negative emotional reactions to them). Most of the gold-standard treatments for anxiety disorders also employ vairagya to help clients let unwanted thoughts and sensations come and go with only minimally anxious reactions. One recent study demonstrated that experience with meditation was associated with an increase in ability to remain calm and free of negative emotional experiences in the face of unwanted thoughts that would otherwise be distressing.

Despite the great increase in interest by Western yoga practitioners and mental health professionals, few good resources exist on the theoretical foundations and methods of yoga-infused psychotherapy. *Healing the Whole Person: Yoga Psychotherapy* is an important resource for both laypersons and professionals alike. Its esteemed author, Swami Ajaya, PhD, a Western-trained psychologist and ordained monk of an ancient Indian order of yogis, provides a thorough general introduction to yoga psychotherapy that will educate and inspire the reader. Mental health professionals who wish to incorporate aspects of yoga into their work with clients will be pleased to find that it is practical and immediately useful, as well as being theoretically enlightening. Hatha yoga practitioners in the general population will also find this book helpful, as it casts a light on yoga as it pertains to the mind, an area neglected by most mainstream hatha instructors. Swami Ajaya's is truly a special voice that has much to offer us in our quest to understand the mind and the psychological foundations of growth and change.

## Monism and Yoga Psychology

Yoga psychotherapy is grounded in Vedanta, a school of monistic Indian philosophy that describes the manifest universe and all that exists beyond as a manifestation of consciousness. It tells us that the individual, like all else, is in essence pure consciousness and that our consciousness/awareness is the only thing about us that does not change. Our thoughts and emotions change from moment to moment. Our deeper beliefs change over time. Our bodies grow and change as well, until such time as they are returned to their constituent elements.

On a practical level that is relevant to yoga psychology and to the helping professions, monistic philosophy suggests that the individual should learn to identify with awareness itself, more so than with the ever-changing contents of awareness. He/she should learn to take on what Gary Emery's Radical Cognitive Therapy (RCT) refers to as the "bird's-eye view" rather than the "worm's-eye view." If we can learn from the contents of awareness (from experience) while remaining a calm and balanced witness, it is suggested that we can not only minimize distress but free up energy for more positive experiences such as love and joy.

Vedanta and yoga psychology also tell us that the human *being* is not simply a personality, a collection of preconditioned internal and external habits and other self-perpetuating patterns, but is actually a higher-order *experiencer* of such finite and changing *things*. As Swami Ajaya explains, the personality is only an environment through which we (our awareness and its intrinsic energy) flow.

Unlike the majority of traditional Western psychotherapies, yoga psychotherapy provides the means, not only for change at the level of personality (that is, at the levels of thought, emotion, behavior, and so on), but for change at a much more profound level. It can teach us to become peaceful, happy, and accepting witnesses of ourselves and the world, under all circumstances, even as we simultaneously struggle to improve ourselves at the level of personality.

Through the application of vairagya, yoga psychotherapy also serves to restore personal choice, freeing up the individual to live his or her life in a more proactive and deliberate way that reflects personal goals and values and not just the force of the most recent emotional winds. Like both ACT and DBT, yoga psychotherapy demonstrates that making peace with a current reality is in no way antithetical to change or growth but is in fact the foundation upon which change takes place. Energy that is at first directed toward resisting uncontrollable internal and external circumstances can be channeled toward more controllable values-based and goal-directed behaviors in order to build happier and healthier lives. Yoga psychotherapy teaches balance, not only for the sake of emotional stability but in order to free up internal resources for action and change. According to an ancient Indian maxim, the flight to the divine—and better mental health—requires two wings: vairagya and sadhana (change-oriented disciplines/behaviors).

## What Yoga Psychotherapy Is Not

There is a great deal of confusion in the West as to the true nature of authentic yoga and, naturally, this extends to yoga-based psychotherapy. To clarify, it will be useful to discuss some of the things yoga psychotherapy is not. First, yoga psychotherapy is not exercise. Many Americans, including a significant number of longtime hatha yoga practitioners and instructors, mistakenly believe that yoga is simply a finite set of stretches and breathing exercises. It is not. While hatha yoga is a valuable part of the larger yoga tradition, it is a relatively recent addition and is limited in scope. It is by far the most popular form of yoga in the West but should not be viewed as its only form.

Both therapists and potential yoga psychotherapy clients should understand that while hatha may be incorporated into treatment as an adjunctive or supportive practice, it does not comprise one of the more central elements of yoga psychotherapy. Yoga psychotherapy targets the mind more directly, through the application of more psychological and spiritual principles and techniques, so as to provide the client with greater self-knowledge and more tools than can be gained in a weekly hatha yoga class, and more quickly. In this regard, it should be understood that yoga psychotherapy does not provide the means for exercising around a problem, without having to address it directly, but is actually the means for honest and direct self-reflection and growth. As with any form of psychotherapy, yoga psychotherapy requires great courage on the part of the client, who must be willing to face his or her problems directly and to work hard at implementing real changes in lifestyle and behavior.

Second, neither traditional yoga nor yoga psychotherapy is New Age. The theories and methods of yoga have been practiced, refined, and experimentally verified over the course of thousands of years and should not be confused with any of the myriad New Age therapies that have sprung up in recent decades. Yoga psychotherapy employs the systematic practices of authentic yoga, as they relate to mental health, and does not involve fads such as astral travel, channeling, or fortune-telling.

Third, yoga psychotherapy is not "spiritual" in some flashy or abstract but impractical way. Like authentic yoga, the principles and methods of yoga psychotherapy should (at least initially) target specific problematic attitudes and behaviors, with an aim to bettering the individual in real, concrete, and practical ways. According to yoga philosophy, we are already perfect in essence, and need only remove the blinders of the lower mind to become truly happy, free, and loving. Yoga psychotherapy targets some of the more problematic modifications of mind referred to by Patanjali, in ways that are specific, practical, and effective.

Fourth, yoga psychotherapy is not religious or dogmatic. Unlike religiosity, which is often associated with poor mental health, authentic spirituality does not require a blind or rigid adherence to any set of socially prescribed and enforced beliefs. The attitudes and methods of yogic spirituality are practiced within all of the great world religions and by millions of others who do not identify with any one religious or social group or organization. They are simply healthy and practical behaviors that help us to relate to our own experiences and do not require the abandonment or adoption of any particular ideology. Further, neither yoga nor yoga psychotherapy is puritanical or punitive. On the contrary, this approach recognizes that people have the right to grow at their own pace and should not punish themselves for not being more "spiritual" or more "disciplined."

Lastly, unlike most forms of Western psychotherapy, Yoga psychotherapy is not simply a means of escaping or minimizing problematic "symptoms." According to yoga, pain is a guru that redirects us from complacency to learning and insight, which constitute the very purpose of life. The problems of human life, while they may be unpleasant, are thus treated as a means for growth and represent opportunities for a lifetime of development. Yoga psychotherapy helps clients to learn from the obstacles that they encounter on their life journeys while teaching them to remain balanced in the presence of obstacles.

### Principles of Yoga Psychotherapy

The word *yoga* is used in reference to an almost mind-boggling number of varied but related philosophies and spiritual disciplines. Many are directly relevant to mental health. In the pages that follow, Swami Ajaya will introduce and discuss some of these tools, the theories behind them, and parallels to Western psychological paradigms and techniques. Here will be elaborated some general principles that apply to yoga psychotherapy and provide context for the specific interventions discussed by Swami Ajaya.

Yoga psychotherapy, as previously noted, is practical and addresses the specific themes and problems that brought the client to therapy. Later in treatment, there may be time for more general philosophizing and intellectual discourse, as clients move from the resolution of specific problems to strategizing for future well-being. Initially, however, treatment should be pragmatic and serve to reduce client suffering. Like the empirically supported treatments of Western psychology, all authentic forms of spirituality emphasize concrete and practical change over simple intellectualizing and theoretical speculation.

While yoga psychotherapy is guided by the principle of practicality and initially targets the specific internal and external conditions responsible for suffering, it is not simply a means to reducing and eliminating suffering. Yoga psychotherapy is also a form of "positive psychology," which has become increasingly popular among forward-thinking mental health professionals. Nearly all Western psychotherapeutic paradigms are similar in that they are designed only to reduce negative experiences, such as depression, panic attacks, psychosis, or marital conflict. Yoga psychotherapy, in contrast, is capable not only of reducing distress due to specific symptom constellations but also provides means for directly increasing the experience of positives, such as love, creativity, and interpersonal connection. It is not the only or even the prevailing form of positive psychology in the West, but it is certainly the oldest and most experimentally refined. Yoga has been serving to increase joy, as well as to reduce suffering, for thousands of years.

Yoga psychotherapy is "holistic" in that it considers and addresses all aspects of the individual and the patterns of relations between them. This holistic approach includes the cognitive, emotional, physiological, behavioral, and interpersonal domains addressed by Western psychology but acknowledges and adds numerous others, such as diet, sleep, breath, and spirituality. Yoga psychotherapy acknowledges that human beings are affected by all aspects of their experience and seeks to identify and remedy any and all habits that may be contributing to distress and/or "dis-ease."

In keeping with both yoga's practicality and its non-dogmatism, yoga psychotherapy is experimental and experiential in application. Clients are asked not simply to speculate about or blindly adopt the "spiritual" ideas and methods of yoga but are encouraged to experiment with the attitudes and methods provided to them. The yoga psychotherapist will never force a new perspective on a suffering client but rather will assist him or her to test the validity and efficacy of specific theories and tools. The goal here is twofold. First, such an approach serves to communicate a deep respect for the individual and his or her right to make decisions for him/herself. Second, taking an experimental approach to change allows the therapist-client team to determine scientifically which methods will be effective for the client, and under what circumstances. The theories of yoga psychology are compelling and may serve as inspiration for clients but are ultimately useless unless one has tested these methods and found them to be helpful.

In addition to being practical in an immediate and tangible way, yoga psychotherapy is practical in a long-term sense, as well. Unlike most Western forms of psychology, yoga psychology is concerned with providing the individual with tools and attitudes that may be used for a lifetime of growth and development. In this sense, yoga psychotherapy is "spiritual." It is not simply a means for creating and maintaining a relatively healthy status quo; it provides the means for a lifetime of balance, learning, and an ever-increasing sensitivity to reality (on relative and absolute levels). In comparison to other types of psychotherapy that are designed only to rescue and return individuals to their previous levels of baseline functioning, psychotherapies that offer only fish, yoga psychotherapy teaches the individual the art of fishing. It helps clients not only to pull out of their current emotional nosedives. It provides the skills necessary for the continuing flight to divinity.

As discussed by Swami Ajaya, yoga psychotherapy teaches the tools required for individuals to understand, negotiate, and transcend the polarities (pairs of complementary forces such as love and hate, success and failure) that characterize each stage of psycho-spiritual development. Whether one is struggling with issues related to physical safety and security, self-worth, impulse control, or interpersonal connections, yoga psychotherapy offers practical strategies to support both current and future learning and problem resolution. Human beings, if they are to reach their fullest potential, must make peace with all of the various polarities that define human life (and death). Yoga shows the way.

Spirituality is neglected by most forms of Western psychology and psychotherapy and is often regarded as a niche specialty without practical application. This is grossly inaccurate and will certainly change as progressive mental health professionals continue to demonstrate the benefits of a spiritual approach to behavior change.

Another notable feature of yoga psychotherapy is its appropriateness for people of all cultures. The methods of yogic spirituality can be located within the context of many different cultures and religions, throughout the history of human civilization. Hindus, Buddhists, Jains, Sikhs, Sufi Muslims, Christian mystics, Kabbalistic Jews, and other nonsectarian yogis have all found yogic spirituality to have significant mental health benefits. The methods have also been used in modern psychotherapies such as ACT and DBT to help clients of a wide variety of ethnicities, nationalities, and religions, thus demonstrating their global appeal and efficacy. It is rare that a single psychotherapeutic approach is appropriate to so many, making yoga psychotherapy even more special a development.

## Attitudes and Techniques

There are numerous yogic attitudes and techniques with direct relevance to mental health. Vairagya, meditation, self-acceptance (not to be confused with the self-esteem construct of Western psychology), mindfulness (i.e., meditation in action), pranayama (breath regulation), and *viveka* (discrimination) constitute some of the more effective and widely applied methods and will be described here.

### Vairagya

Perhaps the most important contribution of yoga psychology is the ancient construct of vairagya. More of a general attitude than a specific technique (with only circumscribed utility), vairagya is both an effective tool in its own right and the foundation upon which numerous other tools rest.

Through the systematic cultivation of a state of non-attraction and non-aversion (what Steven Hayes calls "acceptance"), clients can be taught to remain emotionally balanced and content in the face of all types of stimulus, both internal (thoughts/cognitions, physiological sensations, emotions) and external (environmental conditions, anxiety-provoking objects and situations). This state holds the key not just to overcoming specific fears and sensitivities but to a lifetime of contentment and resilience. Vairagya, when fully cultivated, equals true freedom and allows us to learn from the obstacles encountered on our life journeys without being emotionally hijacked by them.

According to several Western schools of psychodynamic psychology, most individuals respond to external objects (people, places, things, or ideas) and their internal representations in one of three ways—they move toward them (attraction), away from them (aversion), or against them (attraction and aversion). Yoga psychotherapy recognizes the legitimacy of such relations in the subject-object paradigm but offers the means for an important fourth way of "relating" to things. Through vairagya, it offers the means for "simply being" with internal and external objects, peacefully coexisting with them such that a minimum of energy is directed toward them. It is appropriate to move toward, away from, and against objects, in various contexts, but it is vital to well-being that people also learn to peacefully "be" with some objects.

It should be understood that the ongoing practice of vairagya does not constitute a misguided effort at numbness to reality, as it is sometimes misunderstood. In fact, it is intended as a way for one to be fully open and accepting of life as it is (even as efforts are made to improve it with other methods). It allows individuals to experience life fully while remaining balanced in the presence of obstacles, and it ultimately prepares one to perceive reality in its purest form as pure, unadulterated consciousness.

Clinical applications of vairagya (known by various Western names) include a wide variety of related treatments for the anxiety disorders. The scientifically supported, gold-standard treatments for panic disorder, for example, involve teaching clients to accept unwanted thoughts and bodily sensations for what they are, without catastrophizing or frantically trying to escape them. The scientifically indicated treatments of choice for obsessive-compulsive disorder (OCD) also employ vairagya in a highly practical and systematic way. In treating OCD, anxiety specialists progressively expose clients to feared stimuli of increasing intensity while helping them to practice acceptance of the unwanted thoughts and sensations. This allows clients to experience anxiety cues and the resulting anxious sensations in a spirit of acceptance so that they can develop a tolerance for/immunity to them, at which point the stimuli cease to elicit distress. Vairagya is a powerful tool that all humans must eventually learn if they are to find true peace and happiness.

## Meditation

Meditation is the most important of all yogic techniques. Not only does it offer a wide variety of short- and long-term medical and mental health benefits, it offers to its practitioners a lifetime of ever increasing self-awareness and self-control, and ultimately full enlightenment (full awareness of the oneness of all existence). In the words of the great yogi saint Sri Swami Rama of the Himalayas, "[Meditation] is a simple technique of learning to pay attention to and understand all the various levels of ourselves." Such a technique, though simple, thus has the power both to facilitate learning and growth at the level of the mind and to carry a person beyond the confines of the individual mind to absolute consciousness.

As regards mental health, meditation has been shown to produce significant relief for people suffering from a myriad of different conditions—stress, anxiety disorders, and depression, to name a few—and to produce a variety of positive new experiences. In yoga psychotherapy, clients are taught to meditate for four primary reasons. First, it is calming for both the body and mind and is, according to several scientific studies, more relaxing than any other kind of rest. Second, as mentioned above, meditation leads to increased self-awareness, allowing us to make more informed decisions regarding how to deal with our psychological issues. Third, it is said to increase awareness of contingencies operating in the environment and serves to help us in the efficient negotiation of life situations.

An important fourth benefit of meditation, as applied in yoga psychotherapy, pertains directly to vairagya. By sitting still, breathing slowly and evenly, and making an effort to focus on a single point, clients learn to accept and let go of thoughts that would otherwise trigger negative emotional states. One recent correlational study, by the author of this chapter, found that degree of emotional distress over unwanted, intrusive thoughts decreased as degree of experience with meditation increased. Those subjects who had been practicing for more months and years experienced less sadness, less worry, less guilt, and less disapproval (in their thoughts) than those with less meditative experience. Further, they were also less inclined to believe blindly in the contents of their thoughts and were able let them go more quickly.

## Self-Acceptance

Self-esteem is defined by most Western psychologists as the perceived distance between the propositional "ideal" version of oneself and the perceived or actual self. That is to say, when people believe that they are closer to their ideal self, they have greater self-esteem. Likewise, if people believe that there exists a large difference between the real self and the ideal, they will suffer from low self-esteem.

While nearly all yogis would agree that it is better to have high self-esteem than low self-esteem, self-esteem itself is regarded as a flawed and problematic concept in that it is conditional by nature. The ongoing practice of unconditional self-acceptance, in yoga psychotherapy, replaces the conditional construct of self-esteem that is so intrinsic to most Western psychotherapies.

In yoga psychotherapy, clients are taught to eliminate the "middle man" (rules and conditions) and to accept themselves fully (including all of their perceived shortcomings), even as they work to change and improve themselves. According to yoga, we must learn to accept and nurture each subsequent version of the perceived self/personality so as to avoid developing and/or maintaining the terribly unhealthy habits of beating ourselves up and disliking ourselves (for any reason). Beating ourselves up is never good. When we repeatedly engage in the act of self-denigration, a terrible habit is established, and it remains even after we have eliminated or transcended the traits and behaviors that initially triggered the self-abusive behavior. By practicing unconditional self-acceptance of ourselves (and it is a practice!) at all times, regardless of what we have done in the past or the flaws that we may perceive in our present selves, we not only cease to hurt ourselves but free ourselves up to love the self and others (whom we may have also judged and denigrated for traits that we would not have accepted in ourselves).

## Mindfulness

The word *mindfulness* has been defined in a variety of ways by Western mental health professionals. Often it is defined in precisely the same way as vairagya and acceptance and has found significant scientific support (which further attests to the power of vairagya!). Here, a more traditional yogic definition is given. According to the ancient yoga tradition, mindfulness is a construct very closely related to vairagya but is respected as a practice in its own right. It is understood by yogis to be a conscious effort at attention to presenting reality (the accompanying but distinct practice of vairagya provides the balance required to accept the realities perceived through the practice of mindfulness).

Mindfulness, as defined above, is a powerful component of yoga psychotherapy, providing clients with a wealth of new data upon which to base decisions and behavior. Clients are taught to witness/perceive internal and external conditions directly and consequently to reduce their dependence on elaborate cognitive speculation, an indirect way of knowing that is prone to a much greater margin of error than mindfulness. By making efforts toward a continual awareness of our experiences, both internal (thoughts, emotions, physiological sensations) and external (sensory experiences, initiated behavior), we become directly aware of the complex relationships that exist between various experiences. This new awareness allows us to begin detecting and disrupting unhealthy patterns and to begin creating newer, healthier ones. It allows us to effectively manage our internal states and to restore a greater free will regarding behavior.

As noted above, mindfulness is best practiced along with vairagya, and according to some research, is inert without it. If we are not willing to fully accept our previously unknown internal conditions for what they are, it is unlikely that those conditions will be perceived or understood.

## Discrimination (Viveka)

Like modern cognitive-behavioral therapies, yoga psychotherapy also provides tools for examining the accuracy of the thoughts that appear within the field of awareness. Preconceived and conditioned thoughts and beliefs must first be welcomed into consciousness in a spirit of balance and acceptance but may then be examined for validity, as appropriate. Many people suffer needlessly as a result of inaccurate negative thoughts that have been blindly accepted without logical analysis.

Yoga psychotherapy helps clients to refine *buddhi*, the mind's faculty of discrimination, so that they are increasingly able to penetrate *avidya* (ignorance/misperception) as it pertains immediately to mental health. For example, a person who mistakenly believes that he or she is disliked by all might be helped to examine this conclusion rationally by considering the evidence for and against it, as well as any unjustified jumps in reasoning that had supported the incorrect conclusion. As within classical cognitive-behavior therapy, such analytic skills are taught to the client for use outside the therapeutic session but are also practiced within the session, in a Socratic manner. Many clients can be helped simply by liberation from the delusion of inaccurate and poorly examined conclusions. In the words of the great yogi and philosopher Sri Shankaracharya, "As long as our delusion continues, the rope appears to be a snake. When the delusion ends, the snake ceases to exist."

One fundamental difference between the linear rational analysis of cognitive-behaviorism and the viveka of yoga and yoga psychotherapy concerns the limitless utility and ultimate result of viveka. According to yoga, avidya is far more than simply the cause of temporary and conditional suffering (as with a time-limited episode of depression or a panic attack). It is the cause of all suffering in a universal sense and causes human beings, who are in essence pure and infinite consciousness, to believe that they are finite, isolated, and subject to change. By the ongoing practice of discrimination, we may, in time, be freed of all false identifications and come to know ourselves as infinite *satchitananda* (knowledge-existence-bliss), beyond all change and conditions. Discrimination, as taught in yoga psychotherapy, is practical and helps clients to end current suffering due to inaccurate beliefs but also prepares them for a lifetime of spiritual evolution and the ultimate goal of life—enlightenment.

### Pranayama

One very important aspect of human functioning that has been ignored by most of Western psychology is the breath. Consequently, Western psychotherapists have failed to grasp the power of breath-regulation for the improvement of general well-being and for the reduction of suffering due to specific psychological and physiological symptoms. Yoga psychology, on the other hand, recognizes a wide variety of powerful breathing exercises and a very wide variety of conditions for which they are indicated. Through the ongoing practice of pranayamas that are tailored to the individual, it is possible to regulate the activity of the nervous system, leading to a calmer and healthier body and mind.

It is obvious that breathing is related to both states of the body and states of the mind. We have only to mindfully attend to and reflect on the course of daily events to see as much. When we are surprised or startled, we gasp for air. States of anxiety are accompanied by breathing patterns wherein the breath is short, shallow, and fast. Depression is associated with breath that is slow, labored, and broken by long pauses between inhalation and exhalation. States of mind and body characterized by subjective feelings of calmness and contentment are connected with smooth, relaxed, and even breathing, without jerks or pauses.

To address problems with mental health, yoga psychotherapy offers the client specific breathing exercises that target problematic and distressing aspects of experience. For a client suffering from panic attacks, for example, a therapist should prescribe 1:1 diaphragmatic breathing (relaxed breathing through the nose, where the inhalation and exhalation are of equal length and are not broken by jerks or pauses), which calms the autonomic nervous system and prevents the hyperventilation that so frequently triggers and/or maintains the experience of panic. A depressed client, on the other hand, might be asked to practice *khapalabhati,* a breathing exercise involving a quick and forceful exhalation through the nose followed by a slow, natural, and relaxed inhalation (also though the nose). Khapalabhati has long been known to purify the respiratory system for healthier breathing throughout the day, to aid in the elimination of toxins from the body, and to arouse energy (which is absent in depressive states). Other pranayamas also exist to help insomniacs get much-needed sleep and for a myriad of other psycho-physiological issues. Because the pranayamas of yoga and yoga psychotherapy are powerful techniques that act directly on the nervous system, they should be taught by a knowledgeable person, practiced with care, and not be overpracticed so as to produce new imbalances.

The reader will be happy to know that Swami Ajaya also introduces and discusses the exciting and much-talked-about but rarely understood chakra system and its relation to psycho-spiritual evolution. The chakras of the subtle body (the field of energy that permeates the gross body), as described in the texts of the tantric and hatha yoga systems, are a very popular topic among both practitioners of authentic spiritual traditions and members of the New Age community. Unfortunately, the enthusiasm with which the subject is approached is almost never matched with an equal degree of genuine knowledge. In every city in the United States, practitioners of the New Age arts and outsiders to the oral traditions of authentic yoga are writing and lecturing about the flashy topic, generating a great deal of confusion and misinformation about the chakras. This text will stand in stark contrast to the majority of materials available on the subject. Not only is Swami Ajaya a trained scientist with a mind for critical thinking, he is a respected monk of one of the most ancient and reputable orders of yogis and is privy to written and oral knowledge with which most people will never come into contact. Further, he is a longtime practitioner of authentic yoga and has much personal experience with the chakra system.

In *Healing the Whole Person*, Swami Ajaya systematically describes the chakras of the human body and relates them to the specific Jungian archetypes, polarities, and clinical issues that are associated with them. In this way, the reader is given a clear framework for understanding mental health and spiritual development, from the most basic and primal problems of human life to the deepest and most subtle. Also provided is an understanding of how a variety of Western schools of psychology arose to meet the needs of people struggling at different levels of psycho-spiritual development. Most important, Swami Ajaya introduces and discusses some of the tools and attitudes that can be helpful to individuals who are dealing with problems commonly encountered in the process of spiritual evolution.

The renowned yogi monk and clinical psychologist Swami Ajaya is an important voice in modern psychology and one of a small number of true authorities on yoga psychotherapy. It is my hope that you will both enjoy and be informed by the special book that you hold in your hand. Rarely is such a careful and credible treatment of yoga psychology offered directly to the public.

# HEALING the WHOLE PERSON

APPLICATIONS OF YOGA PSYCHOTHERAPY

*Chapter One*

# THE ECOLOGY OF CONSCIOUSNESS

MONISTIC PSYCHOLOGY POSITS THAT CONSCIOUSNESS ALONE IS self-existent and that all else only apparently seems to exist. All distress comes from ignoring the underlying reality and identifying with the world of names and forms. Yoga science studies and explains the way in which a person's consciousness has become absorbed in the world of names and forms and provides the means to lead him out of this ensnarement. Yoga is an ecological science: it attempts to comprehend, in all of its aspects, the environment in which a person is involved, and then to free him from his entanglements.

Modern psychology identifies the human being with his personality and thoughts and considers his environment to be his external surroundings, including the air he breathes and his home and work space. But yoga psychology considers consciousness to be the essence of a person, and all else to be the environment in which consciousness is embedded. In addition to one's external environment, which exists outside of his skin, one has an internal environment, which includes his body, emotions, thoughts, desires, and appetites. In much the same way that a worldly environmentalist would be concerned with restoring a polluted lake to its natural state of purity and equilibrium, the yoga therapist is interested in leading a person from the experience of disturbance to the consciousness of equilibrium and tranquility.

The monistic model is based on two underlying principles; the wide variety of interventions used in yoga therapy is a consequence of the application of those principles. When the principles are clearly understood, the underlying unity behind the apparent diversity of focuses in yoga therapy becomes discernible. The first principle is that self-realization is a process of purification; one has only to remove the impurities and encumbrances that obscure one's true nature as pure consciousness in order to be free of all distress and suffering. The principle of purification runs throughout all the techniques of yoga science and is applied in working with each facet of the human being. Since one is already pure unlimited consciousness, the process of growth consists of discarding all other beliefs and assumptions and recognizing what one is and always has been. Those unreal qualities that one has superimposed upon himself may be regarded as pollutants in much the same way that one regards smoke to be a pollutant of the air. Just as the removal of smoke leaves air pure and uncontaminated, so the removal of limiting self-concepts allows pure consciousness to become unveiled. Yoga therapy in all its phases consists of nothing but the removal of the various pollutants that obscure pure consciousness, which is one's true essence.

Those pollutants are found in various forms and in all aspects of our being. In the ordinary person, each instrument of pure consciousness is encumbered by pollutants. The first phase of yoga science consists of freeing those instruments from the pollutants, enabling them to serve as fit vehicles for the expression of the Self in the manifest world. The body is polluted by toxins it cannot assimilate, and in a similar way the mind is polluted by thoughts that do not reflect the underlying reality. The person identifies with those thoughts, and his awareness of the Self is therefore obscured. But when those pollutants are removed through the practice of meditation, one experiences his true nature.

The second principle of yoga therapy is holism. Yoga science applies the process of purification to each aspect of the human being. The ecological situation in which consciousness finds itself includes a person's living environment, his body and all of its functions, the air he breathes and the food he eats, his relationships and his manner of relating, his emotional and ego states, and his habits, desires, and thoughts. Yoga psychology takes into account all the variables in the world of form, however gross or subtle, that may affect the ability of a human being to be aware of his true nature, and step by step seeks to unravel the complex knots that bind the person to those forms. The entire ecological situation must be considered, including the interconnections between the various aspects of the environment, if one is to become free of the hold that one's internal and external environment apparently has over consciousness. Yoga psychology does not concentrate on one aspect or a few aspects of the human being, but helps consciousness disentangle itself from every facet of its environment. Thus, yoga is truly a holistic science.

## THE HOLISTIC MODEL

Although analytic, atomistic, and reductive theories and methods have predominated in modern psychology and psychotherapy, there have been significant schools of psychology that have stressed the holistic and purposive functioning of the organism. Those schools have come predominantly from the German philosophical tradition. Two such schools that emerged in the first half of this century are gestalt psychology and organismic psychology. Recently the holistic perspective has begun to establish a foothold in modern medicine and psychotherapy. Theorists in this emerging field have attempted to define the basic principles upon which holistic therapy is based.

In the more orthodox Western therapies, mind, body, and spirit are separated into three distinct areas, with specialists to deal with each facet of the human being independently, and with little interaction among the specialists. As a result, it is not unusual for the different specialists treating a person in each of these areas to be working at cross-purposes. However, in the yogic model, medical, psychological, and spiritual needs are dealt with synergistically. The yoga therapist relates to the human being as a whole and seeks to understand how the various aspects of a person function together. A fundamental tenet of yoga therapy is that there is body-mind-spirit integration. Physical functioning, mental functioning, and one's relation to ultimate values and purposes are all of a piece, reflecting one another. The yoga therapist is aware of this interrelationship and leads his client to become aware of it as well. He uses techniques that are effective on each level.

In the medical model followed by the vast majority of physicians in our society today, a specialist treats the organ system in the body through which symptoms are expressed. He may give the patient suppressive drugs that clear up the symptoms in that organ system; but since the underlying disturbance remains untreated, it will continue to develop and sooner or later will express itself through another channel. Furthermore, the pharmaceutical agents that are ingested typically create imbalances in the organism, causing reactions as the organism attempts to adjust or throw off the foreign substance. As a result, additional imbalances are likely to appear in other systems within the organism. These mental, emotional, or physical disturbances are usually considered to be merely annoying and unimportant side effects, but all too often they turn out to be more disturbing to the organism than were the original symptoms. Thus suppressive treatment may result in serious symptoms in other organ systems that neither physician nor patient recognize as being an outcome of the earlier treatment. So the patient goes to another specialist who deals with the organ system now affected and receives another pharmaceutical agent that suppresses the new symptom. This chases the disturbance to still another area and actually has the effect of imbedding the original imbalance more deeply within.

For example, eczema may be treated with symptom-suppressive ointments that seem to be quite effective on the surface: the treatment appears to be successful, and the skin rash clears up. But after some time the patient may develop an asthmatic condition and consult a specialist in respiratory diseases. The patient has no idea that his present respiratory distress is related to his previous skin condition, and unfortunately his physician is probably also unaware of the possibility of there being a connection between the two conditions. A careful study of the two conditions, however, reveals that when either asthma or eczema is treated with suppressive drugs, the other condition often appears. The effect of the suppressive treatment of eczema is to drive the disease deeper within the organism, resulting in an asthmatic condition. An even worse situation is created if treatment of the asthma drives the disease still deeper to a more subtle level of functioning, resulting in mental disturbance. If the asthmatic condition is treated with symptom-suppressive steroids, as it usually is, the natural adaptive functions of the body deteriorate further and result in the atrophy of the adrenal glands, and out of that condition a psychiatric disturbance may emerge. The situation may be even more complex than already described. Strange though it may seem, those who have worked extensively with families have found that the treatment of one family member may lead to the emergence of related symptoms in another member of the same family. It is therefore necessary for a truly holistic model to consider the family as an organism and to be aware of the effects that symptoms and their suppressions have on other family members.

The yoga therapist trains himself to become acutely aware of the interconnection between various facets of human functioning, and he helps his client to become sensitive to himself in the same way. The practice of yoga science leads one to become more attuned to all aspects of functioning and to gradually gain mastery over every aspect of his ecology. The process is akin to learning biofeedback in each area of one's functioning. However, instead of relying on machines to amplify and give him feedback about changes in his internal ecology, the student of yoga learns how to become sensitive to his internal processes without the aid of machines, so that inner changes register more clearly in his awareness. For instance, in the process of learning hatha yoga, one becomes increasingly sensitive to physical tension and discomfort in the body and learns processes of self-regulation to reduce or eliminate those symptoms. He also becomes aware of how his breathing pattern, diet, thinking patterns, habits, and way of relating to others contribute to the physical tension or relax-ation he experiences and how his physical state affects those other aspects of his experience.

The yoga therapist may work together with other profes-sionals who complement his own expertise to jointly provide training for his client. Training in self-awareness and self-regu-lation of the body, diet, breath, habit patterns, emotions, states of mind, values, will, unconscious processes, desires, and rela-tion to archetypal processes and to transcendent being—which are treated in isolation in various therapies—must be integrated in a truly synthetic approach to optimal function-ing. If any area is left out, the therapy is incomplete. Fur-thermore, for treatment to be effective, there must be aware-ness of the way in which intervention at one level of func-tioning affects the other facets, for example, how a change in diet alters the breathing pattern and the mental state. At best, the techniques used at different levels not only complement one another but work synergistically as a unit.

The yoga therapist is not limited to a single modality of therapy, or even to a few: he has a wide array from which to choose. He may meet with a client individually, or he may meet with a couple or with a family. If he has the resources, he may provide a therapeutic environment in which the client can work on various aspects of his functioning—physical, emotional, interpersonal, and spiritual. The ashram or residential environment is a form of milieu therapy in which students can work jointly on expanding self-awareness. This type of environment provides the opportunity for regular practice in each aspect of yoga therapy, including diet, hatha yoga postures, breathing, meditation, solitude, self-study, and ego transcendence. There is also a chance to deal with projections and transference in interpersonal relations. In such an environment, there is frequent consultation with the teacher to help the student deal with the conflicts and difficulties that inevitably occur.

Materialistically oriented practitioners treat primarily the physical organism and behavior, and if internal psychological processes are considered to be significant, they are dealt with along mechanistic lines. Some therapists and physicians are currently enlarging their scope, however, and are paying attention to areas of functioning that had previously been ignored. But no modern approach to treatment works with the various facets of a human being in an integrated way; most so-called holistic therapies focus on just a few facets. Only the monistic model offers the possibility for a truly comprehensive approach to the elimination of human suffering.

In most medical and psychological treatments, the spiritual dimension of life is discounted. And many therapists who consider themselves to be holistically oriented, in the sense that they are aware of the body-mind interaction and of the extent to which physical disorders are actually psychosomatic, do not understand the place of the spiritual dimension of life in holistic treatment. Actually, if we trace the etymology of the word "holistic," we find that it has first and foremost a spiritual meaning and is derived from the same root as the word "holy": "The word 'holistic' is derived from the Greek word *holos*...Holos means the entirety or completeness of a thing and is found throughout the New Testament. The state of wholeness and of health was often equated with salvation; a person who was made whole or who was healed was saved."[1]

The holistic conception is found in the words of Paul: "'May the God of peace Himself sanctify you wholly; and may he preserve you whole and entire:' (literally, 'the whole of you') 'in spirit, and in soul, and in body, without blemish.'"[2]

The dualistic paradigm, in contrast to the reductionist and humanistic paradigms, recognizes the importance of the spiritual dimension of human life, as well as acknowledging the part played by the body and mind in contributing to a state of well-being. But it too falls short of being holistic, for according to dualistic models, becoming whole is an ideal that can never be achieved. In this view, the completely unified functioning of all facets of a human being is unattainable: the human being must always remain incomplete; there is always something more that is yet to be integrated. Such a conception is inevitable in the dualistic perspective. In fact, it is its very basis. For if complete integration could be achieved, the conception would not be dualistic, but monistic. The very word "dualism" implies a basic split and therefore an orientation that is not truly holistic.

The monistic model, however, is based on the assumption that unity alone exists. All functioning and all facets of the human being are guided and integrated by that unity. In the monistic paradigm, unity already exists within the person and needs only to be uncovered and recognized, whereas in all other paradigms unity does not and cannot exist. In the other paradigms, the therapist can only approximate a holistic attitude by understanding the way in which certain diverse aspects of a person are functioning in some interrelated way. Only the nondual paradigm is truly holistic.

## DIMENSIONS OF YOGA THERAPY

Yoga is a vast science. Its therapeutic applications cannot be fully encompassed in this volume. To describe each facet of yoga therapy in depth would be, at the least, an encyclopedic undertaking. What follows in this book is merely a small sampling of some of the main aspects of yoga therapy. The way in which the various facets of a human being are dealt with in yoga therapy will be described, beginning with the more material aspect of human existence and progressing toward the more spiritual. When appropriate, illustrations from actual therapy sessions are given.

The content of each psychotherapy session originates primarily from the client: the therapist is responsive to the client's immediate needs and issues. The therapist does not usually respond with didactic teaching, although he may do so occasionally at the request of the client. As is appropriate to the symptoms or issues raised by the client, the therapist at times focuses on body work, breathing techniques, diet, biofeedback, or meditation, but training and practice in such areas is usually not the primary focus of the psychotherapy. Often, but not always, a client working with a yoga therapist has been learning hatha yoga, correct breathing, meditation, and other yogic techniques in classes and is practicing each day outside of the therapy session. The yoga therapist may occasionally help the client to overcome obstacles or refine his practices in those areas. He often works together with holistically oriented physicians, yoga instructors, and other professionals. The psychotherapy itself usually focuses on the psychological and spiritual concerns of the client. The emphasis may be on developing ego strength, dealing effectively with concerns related to sex, work, and eating, changing habit patterns, improving interpersonal relations, resolving inner conflicts, developing self-acceptance, transcending limited identifications, understanding one's purpose in life, or cultivating an awareness of the transcendent.

# Chapter Two

# BODY AND BEHAVIORAL TECHNIQUES

## DIET

AT SOME POINT IN THE PROCESS OF YOGA THERAPY, clients may begin to change their dietary habits. Diet is being discussed first in this section, not because it occupies the central place in psychotherapy based on the yogic model, but because it most clearly illustrates the approach to purification, which is the basis of yoga therapy in working with each aspect of human functioning.

If the client is to experience physical, emotional, and mental ease and comfort, his body needs to be free of contaminants and intoxicants. When one has a cold or influenza, he becomes acutely aware of the effects that toxins in his body can have on all aspects of his functioning. He feels restless and ill at ease; he has difficulty concentrating and experiences other mental and emotional disturbances. In a similar but more subtle way, if one absorbs chemical additives in his food or ingests stimulants or intoxicating drugs that upset his internal chemical balance, his mental and emotional equilibrium will be disturbed. The effects of stimulants and additives can be seen most readily in hyperactive children, many of whom begin to behave normally when put on a pure and natural diet.

Yoga science divides food into three categories: those that create restlessness and disturbance (*rajasic* foods), those that create lethargy and dullness (*tamasic* foods), and those that lead to a peaceful, joyful, relaxed yet energetic state (*sattvic* foods). The client may be encouraged to slowly eliminate foods that leave toxins in his system and that create disturbances and to eat a more pure and natural diet. He may be further encouraged to work with other professionals who are more knowledgeable about the effects of diet and nutrition or who can assess deficiencies in his biochemical makeup and guide him in correcting them. Work in this area can have a profound effect on personality, mood, and cognitive functioning.

The following comments by a young man in yoga therapy illustrate the way that diet can affect one's emotional state and the way he relates to others. This excerpt also points out that discussing and making changes in one's diet can be a meaningful component in psychotherapy.

Yesterday I fixed myself a heavy breakfast. About an hour afterward, I became sluggish and depressed and I was totally despondent for the rest of the day. The energy wasn't in my work. After work when I was driving home, I was screaming, "What's wrong with me?" I felt like my system was messed up in some way, and I was crying. Today I've had only juice. That helped quite a bit; my work went fantastic and I was very friendly with the people that I work with.

I feel I've messed up a lot of relationships. I was talking with a girl yesterday and I was weak and irritable. I want to be consistent; I don't want to be snappy with anyone. Today I felt like going over to where she works. I felt I could be very friendly and energetic and have a real good time. If I could feel generally like I do today, I think my personal relationships will work better. I won't be dwelling on myself; I'll start thinking about the other person.

I'm going to test myself with different foods. Tomorrow I think I'll make a light soup and see how I feel. I stayed off wheat for a long time and then ate it to see how it would affect me because I heard that wheat can cause allergies. I need to do that more—go by my own experiments, not by what Joe Blow says with his latest diet. In the past, I would watch my diet for a week, and then I would pig out and feel miserable. This time I'm going to stick to it and watch what happens. After we talked about my liver last week, I also began paying more attention to that part of my body. I noticed that sometimes I get a sharp pain down there after I eat certain things.

All too often therapists ignore dietary imbalances that may be drastically affecting a client's emotions and behavior. The yoga therapist helps his client become more aware of the way that specific foods affect his physical functioning, his personality, energy level, thinking process, and relationships.[1]

## BODY-MIND INTERACTIONS

Working with the body is an important part of yoga. Body language has been thoroughly studied by yoga psychology, which analyzes all the postures, gestures, and movements found in both animals and human beings. The yoga therapist observes these characteristics in his clients as clues to their inner states. Many people mistakenly associate the word "yoga" with body work alone. Conversely, an equally large group of people think of yoga as a means of reaching a state of consciousness that transcends awareness of the body. But yoga leads neither to preoccupation with nor disregard for the physical level of being. Rather it seeks to optimize functioning at this level in order to free one from identification with the physical being and to bring the physical into harmony with more subtle levels of existence. The yoga therapist helps one to transform his physical being and behavior through such means as proper diet and postural and behavioral techniques, but yoga does not create an entire philosophy and worldview based on the physical level of existence alone: it uses physical and behavioral methods in a way that is integrated with and respectful of more subtle levels of functioning.

Tension carried in the body is intimately related to emotional and mental tension. When one learns to stretch and relax muscles that have been chronically tensed, he experiences a state of relief and ease that he may not have experienced since youth. Each person develops his own characteristic defensive patterns that are expressed in posture, movement, and chronic tension in specific parts of the body. One person may have hunched shoulders, another a rigid chest, a third may pull in his abdomen, and so on. Wilhelm Reich, who studied this subject in depth, used the term "character armor" to refer to the way we chronically tense particular parts of the body in an attempt to protect ourselves:

> Reich asserted a functional identity between the individual's character structure and his muscular armoring—that is, the armoring is the character structure in its physical form. Therefore if one can break down the armoring, one will to the same degree change the neurotic character structure. But since the rigidity of the character is locked into the body, in the armoring, it is more effective to loosen the armoring than to try to change neurotic character traits by forms of talking-out therapy like psychoanalysis.[2]

The practice of hatha yoga leads to effects similar to those attained through such diverse psychophysical disciplines as bioenergetics, chiropractic, Rolfing, and massage. The character armor is gradually broken down through the sustained practice of hatha yoga postures (asanas), and the emotional blocks that accompany characterological muscle tension also give way. As one stretches and relaxes muscles usually held tense, he experiences relief from tension in all aspects of his being. He learns to let go and to trust, becoming aware of a new sense of comfort within. One becomes more in touch with himself at all levels through the practice of hatha yoga.

As he learns to pay more attention to his experience of his body while he maintains a posture, he becomes increasingly sensitive to the body's tensions and its dis-ease. He experiences physical relaxation and the emotional and mental states that accompany this relaxation.

The following excerpt taken from a therapy session with a woman in her mid-thirties illustrates the awareness of body-mind integration that can occur as a result of practicing yoga asanas and discussing one's experiences in the context of yoga therapy.

I have felt very stiff in the last few months, but yesterday I went to a yoga class and I was really amazed at what I was doing. I realized that I have been holding myself back. At times I have the feeling that my hamstrings have been very tense; there is some sort of blockage in the back of the knees, in the hamstrings. I'm very conscious of what I show in front, but the whole back area from my thighs down past my knees is an unconscious part of me. I'm not conscious of it, and I imagine that no one else is conscious of it. I have bad circulation in that area, too.

I wonder if the tension there is related to my wanting to kick? Lately I have been feeling a sense of pent-up rage inside of me. Soccer is the only sport I like to play. When I was younger, I kicked a lot when I fought. My sister would hold me down, but I used to pull hair and kick.

Another woman reported:

When I was in my teens, my shoulders and hips were in proportion; later I became very narrow in the shoulders and wider in the hips. My shoulders became very tight, as though I became ashamed of my breasts, my femininity. In yoga I've opened my shoulders more. Since I've been working with you and doing yoga, my body has gone through some changes. I have a different type of body, more womanly.

The greatly enhanced sensitivity to inner processes and the experience of serenity that come with the practice of hatha yoga encourage one to make changes in other facets of his life, bringing about a greater sense of well-being. For instance, one may become keenly aware of the aftereffects of eating rich foods on his physical, cognitive, and emotional states, and as a result begin to change his diet. Or he may more readily tune in to the physical and emotional discomfort that results from a conflict-based transaction with another person. This awareness can be the first step toward making changes in that relationship so he can maintain the feeling of well-being he has learned to cultivate through yoga.

According to yoga science, posture is an expression of a psychological state. Modern psychologists know that a person's posture can tell a great deal about his inner feelings and his attitudes about himself and others. But psychologists are not generally aware that by purposefully assuming a certain posture, one can induce a particular psychological state. Each of the postures practiced in yoga brings about a particular mental-emotional state in the person who is maintaining the posture. While one posture promotes receptiveness, another may lead to an attitude of superiority. Other postures can help one develop various qualities such as fortitude, steadiness, vigor, equilibrium, humility, balance, and courage.

If one seriously practices asanas and studies their origin and symbolism, he also discovers that yoga postures are actually enactments of archetypal modes of being. In maintaining a prescribed posture, the student brings forth the expression of a particular archetype. Hatha yoga teaches the posture of attainment, the posture of prosperity, the posture of the teacher, the hero's posture, and many more. Assuming one of these postures brings about the corresponding attitude and mode of experience in the yoga student. One's repeated practice of a posture leads to greater awareness and integration of that mode of expression in different aspects of his being.

Along with physical postures, yoga therapy employs relaxation exercises that involve concentration on specific muscles and parts of the body as one consciously relaxes those body parts. There is a series of exercises leading to progressively more subtle and complete states of relaxation. Many of the more elementary techniques of yoga relaxation have been adopted by behaviorally oriented schools of modern therapy, but the techniques that lead to the deeper levels of relaxation are unknown to modern psychology.

Yoga relaxation exercises are effective in the modern world in reducing anxiety and psychosomatic complaints and in releasing repressed emotionality. Such techniques enhance a parasympathetic nervous system response to acute and chronic anxiety. With the use of these relaxation techniques, one can acquire the ability to remain calm and alert despite his external surroundings or internal thoughts. Emotional arousal requires nervous system response, and if the nervous system is trained to remain balanced, disruptive emotional states will not occur. Thus the individual can learn to be less reactive and to more quickly recover a state of equilibrium following an emotional reaction.

Biofeedback training, which has sometimes been called Western yoga, is a helpful adjunct to relaxation training. Some psychologists say that it may simply constitute an elaborate method for teaching relaxation. Biofeedback involves the use of electronic instrumentation to amplify the subject's internal autonomic functioning, thereby making him immediately aware of it. With this kind of training, also known as visceral learning, one eventually learns to recognize tension and relaxation in the body and to use "passive volition" to attain a state of relaxation. In yoga one learns to become increasingly sensitive to internal states so that he can regulate them without the aid of amplifying devices. When one is relatively insensitive to inner processes, electronic instrumentation may be helpful, but as one gradually becomes more keenly aware of inner processes through the continued practice of various aspects of yoga, he goes beyond what can be differentiated or measured by such instruments. Regardless of the relaxation intervention employed, the same basic breathing pattern eventually emerges. This relaxed breath pattern is slower, deeper, smoother, and more abdominal than breathing in other states. Thus the breath can be viewed as an organic mobile biofeedback device, a readily available indicator of autonomic nervous system activity. From time immemorial yogis have known how to use their breathing—and numerous other systems as well—to monitor and regulate such activity.

Relaxation may be learned by the client in separate classes or individual training sessions, but it is sometimes also useful in the therapeutic session itself. A short period of sitting quietly to practice the relaxed breathing pattern, or relaxation in a supine position, may help the client to become centered within himself and more aware of issues and emotions lurking just beneath the surface. It is sometimes helpful for the therapist to guide a client through a relaxation technique and to help him discover areas of tension in the body that are related to emotional issues. One young woman, for example, who always spoke with a soft high voice, complaining that others did not accept her, was led through a relaxation practice by a yoga therapist. There was considerable tension apparent in the throat area, and more time was accordingly spent in relaxing this area. When the tension was released, the young woman experienced a surge of tears and subsequently discussed the lack of self-worth that she feels and how she creates situations that prevent others from nurturing her. Thus the relaxation exercise helped her to experience her emotions more clearly and facilitated her ability to realize and openly deal with her own responsibility in creating her experience of not being accepted.

## BREATH

Breathing is one of the most neglected aspects of human functioning in modern therapy. There are, of course, inhalation therapists who attempt to treat severe disorders in breathing, such as chronic emphysema. But respiratory therapy by itself is incomplete; indeed, it does not even attempt to deal with more than its own very select area of concern. Some psychotherapists teach the rudiments of breath awareness in relaxation training, and those trained in bioenergetics, rebirthing, and Rolfing teach their clients to become aware of and alter their breathing patterns. But there is almost no focus on breathing in most approaches to psychotherapy; there is little awareness that the way one breathes affects all aspects of his life. Breath is the vehicle that links all facets of one's functioning; breathing, posture, and thinking are interrelated, and they influence one another. In yoga psychology, the breath is a tool for regulating all of one's emotional and mental states, and even the way in which one behaves.

Most people take the process of breathing for granted; they assume that breathing is a natural process that need not be given any special attention. But this is not so. Very young children breathe with little inhibition or disturbance of natural breathing rhythms. But as one grows up, he experiences traumas, imitates others, follows erroneous advice, and thereby develops incorrect breathing habits. These lead to chronic distortions in the breathing pattern and consequently to disequilibrium in other functions. Most adults breathe irregularly or they chronically tense some of the muscles involved in the breathing process. A child may develop the habit of raising his shoulders and collapsing his chest in response to frightening situations. If he is often frightened, this may become a chronic posture accompanied by a distortion of his breathing process. A soldier may be taught to stick out his chest and pull in his stomach in order to look more manly. A teenage girl may likewise learn to keep her stomach pulled in to appear more attractive. In each case, a habit is superimposed on the natural breathing process and this alters the process and in turn affects one on many levels, including his physical health and personality.

Swami Vivekananda has said: "The breath is like the fly-wheel of this machine, the body. In a big machine you find the flywheel moving first, and that motion is conveyed to finer and finer parts until the most delicate and finest mechanism in the machine is in motion. The breath is that flywheel, sup-plying and regulating the motive power to everything in this body."[3] If the motion of the flywheel is not regulated, the motion of the entire machine is disturbed. The breath affects more than the body, for the rhythms of the body in turn affect one's emotional and mental life. In yoga science, the breath is considered to be the main link between body and mind.

It has long been accepted that emotions affect the breath-ing process; indeed, people commonly ascertain the emotional states of others by observing such breathing patterns as gasp-ing, sighing, sobbing, laughing, and yawning. It is becoming equally clear that breathing patterns affect emotionality, and an increasing number of studies have been carried out to investigate this understanding, which has always been integral to yoga science. Scientists have verified that the slightest change in respiration induces changes in the rest of the auto-nomic nervous system, and that physiological reaction is an essential component in emotionality.

Respiration affects the right vagus nerve, which in turn controls the autonomic nervous system, and this system regu-lates the secretion of adrenaline, thyroxin, and other hormones of the body. The secretion of these hormones plays a major role in creating one's emotional states. By learning to effect changes in the autonomic nervous system through con-scious alteration of the breathing pattern, one can modify autonomic arousal and modulate subsequent levels of emo-tionality. A few schools of modern psychology and physio-therapy utilize this concept. For instance, Alexander Lowen, who helped to establish bioenergetic therapy, has stated, "Breathing creates feelings, and people are afraid to feel... Inadequate respiration produces anxiety, irritability, and ten-sion... The inability to breathe normally [is] the main obstacle to the recovery of emotional health."[4] The respected physio-therapist Magda Proskauer has declared that "the breath forms a bridge between the conscious and unconscious. Our breathing pattern expresses our inner situation."[5]

When one begins to pay close attention to the breath, the link between breath and emotions becomes obvious. One can readily observe that whenever he or another person becomes emotional, the breath becomes erratic. Emotions such as anger, depression, and fear all have their characteristic patterns of irregular breathing. When one is angry, he tends to hold the breath after inhaling, while depression is often characterized by deep sighs and long pauses after exhalations. Through yoga, one learns to consciously alter his breathing and thus his emotional state.

There are many yogic breathing exercises, each of which achieves specific, well-defined results. Breathing techniques have been developed with a wide range of effects, such as increasing the amount of oxygen in the blood, raising or lowering blood pressure, or promoting relaxation. There are also breathing techniques that induce altered states of consciousness. Yoga therapists have experimented with the effects of breath regulation and have found that striking improvements in one's emotional state can be produced by regulating the breath. For instance, one can attain a calm and alert state through smooth and even diaphragmatic breathing. A client who finds himself becoming emotional in his day-to-day activities may be taught to breathe slowly, deeply, and evenly. He is likely to be surprised at how simple it is to gain control over even intense emotions through this means. Clients often report that when they practice slow, even breathing at a time when they are angry or upset, they find themselves becoming quite calm within only a minute or two. This technique does not lead to the repression of one's emotions but to the ability to witness the emotional part of oneself and regulate it, rather than remaining identified with the emotional state.

Many yogic breathing techniques lead one toward deep

relaxation. One of the first methods taught to a beginning student of yoga is diaphragmatic breathing. This is a key factor in teaching a person to relax physically and mentally and in helping one to become cognizant of feelings that have been held outside of awareness. Here is an excerpt from a therapy session that focuses on this issue:

C: *I had a rough time this week. You suggested that I pay attention to the way I breathe, and it was very difficult. I've been crying a lot. It's related to my mother, I think. I've often had the fantasy that when I was a fetus, her intestines were like a rope which became entangled around my neck and choked me. She didn't want the pregnancy. Later, as I was growing up, I had a tightness in my throat and my breathing was very irregular. I'm breathing better now, but every now and then I feel like I'm suffocating, like I'm choking; I can't get the air in. At other times, I feel a catch in my breath.*

T: *Have you tried to change the way you are breathing?*

C: *I don't have any system. I don't know how to change it yet.*

At this point the therapist taught the client a breathing exercise to be practiced at home. The exercise includes relaxation of the abdominal muscles and diaphragmatic breathing. After practicing this exercise for a few minutes in the therapy session, the client reported:

C: *I'm afraid to be relaxed. I remember often being complimented as a girl because I used to have a very flat stomach and a very thin waist. I was holding everything inside.*

T: *Was your stomach tense?*

C: *It must have been. My stomach was very hard. There was always a fear of being relaxed. I was always anxious. Even now I'm wanting to please. I become anxious trying to please.*

T: *What would it be like if you weren't trying to please?*

C: *I'd be more relaxed. I'd just let go and be able to be myself instead of looking for approval all the time; I'd lose a certain anxious self-consciousness. I've had an image in my mind that for a woman to be attractive, she has to have a flat stomach, but I'm beginning to learn that it's okay to be relaxed and to have the stomach sticking out. When the stomach is relaxed, is it naturally sticking out? I'm so used to it being the other way that relaxing doesn't feel natural.*

T: *Have you ever watched children when they breathe? Do their stomachs stick out?*

C: *It is loose. That is the way it is naturally, I assume. They have a pulsation there with their stomach.*

T: *It might be useful for you to observe yourself breathing in front of a mirror. My sense is that when you hold your stomach in, it also holds in and inhibits feelings.*

C: *I realize that when I relax my abdomen, I feel more sensuous. It's like the difference between the ballerina and the belly dancer. Certainly the belly dancer is more sensuous looking, more human looking.*

T: *In ballet you were taught to hold in the stomach?*

C: *Very much so. If you stick out, the teacher comes and pushes it in. I was really very good at it. My stomach was the flattest.*

Later in this session, the therapist and client went on to explore the client's relationship with her mother and the intense anger that was being kept inside through tensing her diaphragm and inhibiting her breathing.

Alexander Lowen, in describing irregularities in breathing that are related to emotional disorders, commented that, "most people are poor breathers. Their breathing is shallow, and they have a tendency to hold their breath in any situation of stress. Even in such simple stress situations as driving a car, typing a letter, or waiting for an interview, people tend to limit their breathing. The result is to increase their tension."[6] In order to breathe more fully, one must learn to properly empty the lungs with each exhalation. Most people, and particularly neurotic individuals, fail to exhale fully. Lowen found that "the neurotic person finds it difficult to breathe out fully. He holds onto his reserve air as a security measure. Breathing out is a passive procedure; it is the equivalent of 'letting go.' Full expiration is a giving in, a surrender."[7]

Yoga employs an exercise called the complete breath to teach one how to correct for shallow breathing, to inhale and exhale fully, and to increase his breathing capacity. In practicing this exercise, one learns to become aware of each of the muscles used in the process of breathing. After exhaling completely, there is a slow, deliberate inhalation, beginning with the lowering of the diaphragm and continuing as one gradually expands his chest and finally raises the shoulders to completely fill the lungs with air. The process is then reversed with a step-by-step deliberate and complete exhalation. This slow complete breathing may be repeated for some minutes as needed or desired throughout the day.

As mentioned, particular breathing irregularities are associated with specific emotional and psychosomatic disorders. For instance, those experiencing depression or asthma are found to be breathing primarily through their left nostril, and a person who is anxious or restless tends to have a right nostril predominance. Usually simple postures or breathing exercises can easily correct such imbalances. Clinical research has led to the conclusion that six to ten percent of the people seen in medical outpatient clinics are actually suffering from chronic hyperventilation that usually goes undetected.[8] The symptoms described by these patients include dizziness, headaches, chest pains, anxiety, panic attacks, exhaustion, and a variety of physical and emotional complaints. Typically, the physician can find no physical cause for the complaints because the basis is an imbalance in the oxygen/carbon dioxide ratio in the blood, and the physician does not test for this imbalance. Such patients often go from one doctor to another without receiving medical treatment and acquire a reputation as hypochondriacs. They may eventually be referred to a psychiatrist for what is considered to be a hypochondriacal or hysterical disorder. But the symptoms can easily and quickly be erased simply by learning diaphragmatic breathing and an altered ratio of inhalation and exhalation. In a few training sessions, a chronic malady can be easily corrected.[9]

There are many subtle variations in the way human beings breathe. Some people characteristically breathe in slowly and deeply and breathe out in a quick spurt; others breathe in quickly and exhale deliberately. Some inhale or exhale through the mouth, while other individuals hold the breath momentarily at certain points in the breath cycle. One's pattern of breathing is as unique as one's handwriting. The breath may vary along several dimensions from one individual to another or from one time to another in the same individual. These dimensions include: (1) the ratio of inhalation to exhalation, (2) the evenness or unevenness of the air flow, (3) the degree of pause at the end of exhalation or inhalation, (4) the muscles that are used to expand and contract the lungs, (5) the nostril through which the air predominantly moves, (6) the depth of the breath, (7) the frequency of breaths, (8) the force of the exhalation, and (9) the pattern of air flow through the nostrils. As part of the systematic self-observation carried on in yoga science throughout the centuries, the subtle variations in breathing and their effects on all aspects of one's being have been studied in great depth.

In therapy sessions, when a client becomes emotional, his breath may become shallow, with frequent pauses. Such a change is not likely to be observed by a therapist who is not trained in the science of breath, but would be apparent to a yoga therapist. As with diet and body work, breathing techniques may be learned outside of the psychotherapy sessions. However, there are occasions when the breath may become the focus of a therapeutic session. The yoga therapist notices if a client's breathing becomes shallow, if he is tensing the diaphragm and breathing with his chest, if he is holding his breath momentarily. When the therapist becomes aware of irregularities in the client's breathing, he may call attention to those irregularities in order to make the client aware of them. The therapist and client can then explore the relationship between the client's breathing and his emotional or mental states. The therapist may then instruct him in a particular breathing exercise that can help correct the irregularity.[10]

## HABITS

Behavior change is an important component of the process of self-transformation through yoga therapy. Yoga psychology has long recognized that habits play a major role in maintaining one's characteristic behaviors. The human personality is composed of habit patterns, and without changing those patterns the personality cannot be transformed. Most strong and deep-rooted habits are in the unconscious. Since one's habit patterns are outside of one's awareness, it is difficult to break them. Helping a client to change habit patterns constitutes a significant part of yoga therapy.

Most people try to change habits through the use of willpower. They attempt to deny the habit expression, and thereby create a battle within themselves. For instance, if one wants to give up drinking coffee, he will deny himself, and a struggle will ensue between the part of the person that desires to repeat the previous behavior that brought satisfaction and the part of the person that does not want to continue a behavior that he believes is harmful. Typically, there is a tug-of-war, with one side or the other gaining an uncertain advantage. Lasting change does not usually result when one attempts to alter habits in this way.

A theory of the way in which habits become established and how they can be permanently modified has been offered by Patanjali in the *Yoga Sutra*. In the yogic approach to self-transformation, one does not concentrate on the undesirable habit that creates obstacles in his unfoldment. Instead, he turns his attention to establishing a more desirable habit in its place: he repeatedly engages in a new behavior that is incompatible with and antithetical to the undesirable habit. Practicing a new antithetical habit does not allow one to continue the old incompatible habit pattern. This understanding is the key to eliminating undesirable habits.

In the first stages of establishing a new practice, one may have intense desires to engage in the unwanted behavior that he previously found rewarding in certain respects. However, as he continues to practice and find satisfaction in the new habit, his memory of the pleasure gained through the old routine fades, and with it, the attachment of the old habit pattern. For example, if one has been in the habit of drinking each evening but now begins to meditate at night, he will initially experience conflict in giving up his accustomed pleasure and establishing a new routine. While meditating, he may have intermittent intense desires to carry on his usual habit of drinking. But if he perseveres and continues to faithfully meditate, this practice may bring new satisfactions, and the attachment to drinking as a means of finding pleasure will diminish or be eliminated. The *Yoga Sutra* is explicit in describing the necessary conditions for practice to firmly establish a new habit pattern. The *Yoga Sutra* says that one should be fully committed to the new practice and should practice consistently for a considerable period of time.

To be successful in this approach, it is important to find a new practice that provides considerable satisfaction. That makes it easier for one to eliminate the old behavior. For instance, each time one wants a cup of coffee, he might sub-stitute another hot drink, and if he finds a new drink that is genuinely satisfying, the desire for coffee will diminish and eventually all but disappear. As a result of consistent practice, the new and more favorable habit becomes established, and the undesirable habit is extinguished.

This ancient procedure, which underlies the concept of practice in all aspects of yoga, has its modern counterpart in the reciprocal inhibition techniques used by behavior thera-pists. In modern behavior therapy, the client may be placed in anxiety-provoking situations and taught to practice relax-ation. Since the new response—relaxation—is incompatible with the experience of tension, the person ceases to react to the stressful situation with anxiety. In this regard the approaches in yoga therapy and in modern behavioral therapy are similar; however, yoga psychology extends the application of this principle to a much broader range of habits. Yoga psy-chology uses this approach to change behavior of all sorts but also goes beyond a focus on behavior to modify habits of thought as well. In the past few years, behavioral psychologists have also expanded their approach to work with changes in cognitive habits.

Any unwanted habitual behavior, attitude, emotion, or thought pattern that the client has may be altered by culti-vating a new habit incompatible with the first. Thus the yoga therapist may offer specific practices to replace the client's undesirable habits. It is not unusual for the yoga therapist to give his client "homework" or "prescriptions" for behavior to be practiced between therapy sessions. The prescriptions given by a yoga therapist are usually specific to a particular behavior that the client wishes to change. The therapist may ask the client to keep a journal and thus monitor the extent to which he is practicing the new behavior and the results that come from his practice. The client and therapist can then review what occurred and modify the practice to deal with any difficulties.

While one facet of yoga therapy focuses on helping a person to change habit patterns, another aspect teaches a person to transcend the conditioning process. Modern psychology has amply demonstrated that reward and punishment play a major role in the development and maintenance of habits. A person ordinarily follows those routines that bring him reward and avoid punishment. The practice of meditation helps one to more fully experience the present moment and to let go of anticipations of reward and punishment, and in yoga therapy sessions one also learns to give up addictions and aversions and thereby become free of the effects of punishment and reward. One begins to act in the moment rather than being preoccupied with the consequences of his action. The *Bhagavad Gita* advises: "Set thy heart upon thy work, but never on its reward. Work not for a reward...how poor those who work for a reward!"[11] The student of yoga psychology learns to attend to the action itself, to act with awareness, care, and attention. As a result, his acts become more successful. Instead of viewing the current situation as a means to a future end, he uses each circumstance to become more aware, more conscious. He learns to transcend the polarity of success and failure. Here is an example of a client who is cultivating this way of being:

> In the past, I've felt that happiness or sadness is based on what happens, good or bad. Today I was working on a different attitude, allowing what happens externally to be okay, no matter what it is. I'm just maintaining a good feeling and it's not affected by failure or success. Today there was no fear of failure at all, and consequently I just said all kinds of things that I've never been able to say. I did my best at work and I had my boss's best interest in mind, but I wasn't afraid of what he was going to say to me. I was more aware of what we had in common rather than being aware of him being a vice president and judging me.

## TRANSCENDING POLARITIES

Many theorists agree that the basis of suffering is one's experience of being split into conflicting factions. Jung declared that neurotic suffering is the result of inner polarization. "Neurosis," he asserted, "is an inner cleavage—the state of being at war with oneself. Everything that accentuates this cleavage makes the patient worse, and everything that mitigates it tends to heal him. What drives people to war with themselves is the suspicion or the knowledge that they consist of two persons in opposition to one another. The conflict may be between the sensual and the spiritual man, or between the ego and the shadow. It is what Faust means when he says: 'Two souls, alas, are housed within my breast.'"[12] Theories differ in the way they conceptualize the fundamental or typical splits within the person. Psychoanalysis focuses on the conflict between the id and superego, while gestalt therapy is concerned with the conflict between top dog and underdog. Transactional analysis deals with parent, adult, and child ego states, while psychosynthesis helps one to resolve conflicts between subpersonalities. Still other theorists have concerned themselves with the split between a person's verbal and non-verbal communication.

Psychotherapy based on yoga psychology is also concerned with healing the divisiveness that can occur within a person, as well as the divisiveness between oneself and others. Only psychotherapy based on the monistic paradigm can heal all the splits that occur within and without. All other therapies assume a fundamental unhealable division as a result of the assumptions on which the theories are based, but the monistic model leads to a truly unified consciousness. Each of the various means used in yoga therapy is directed toward this end.

The two initial steps in the system known as raja yoga or ashtanga yoga consist of ten principles. The first five, which constitute the first step, deal with interpersonal relations.

These are non-injury, non-lying, non-stealing, non-sensuality, and non-greed. Next come five principles of internal purification: purity, contentment, austerity, self-study, and devotion.[13] If one makes a commitment to follow any one of these ten principles, he will sooner or later realize that it leads away from dualistic consciousness and toward a consciousness based on the recognition of unity. While many aspects of yoga therapy lead one first to understanding and subsequently to a change in behavior, working with these ten principles brings about a change in the other direction: one first modifies his behavior, and that leads to a change in his understanding. Old behavior patterns that lead one to experience duality and conflict (lying, stealing, and so on) are systematically replaced with new behaviors that manifest harmony and unity. Learning and working with these principles can be a significant part of the process of yoga therapy.

In order to better understand how this process works, let us consider the practice of non-lying. This principle has many parallels in modern psychotherapy. Leading theorists have noted that being dishonest with oneself and with others is at the root of both neurotic and schizophrenic functioning. For instance, Helmuth Kaiser advanced the theory that duplicity is "necessary and sufficient for the existence of neurotic disturbance."[14] More recently, Virginia Satir asserted that "the troubled families I have known all have handled their communication through double-level messages."[15] Both Kaiser and Satir have shown that in disturbed communication there is a discrepancy between verbal (conscious) and nonverbal (unconscious) expression, whereas in healthy communication verbal and non-verbal expression are unified and one is fully behind what is being expressed. Healthy communication is characterized by what Satir calls "leveling."

The message is single and straight.
...It represents a truth of the person at a moment in time.
...The position is one of wholeness and free movement. This response is the only one that makes it possible to live in an alive way, rather than a dead way.[16]

In their book *The Structure of Magic*,[17] Richard Bandler and John Grinder point out that disturbed functioning involves deletions and distortions both in one's communications and in the way that one represents the world to himself. After analyzing the therapy of Satir, Peris, and others, Bandler and Grinder concluded that the therapist functions to correct those deletions and distortions in the patient's communications and thereby changes his inner world of experience as well. In most forms of modern therapy, the development of self-honesty and honesty in communication is at the core of the therapeutic process. It is also central to the process of self-transformation in yoga.

In working with the principle of non-lying, the yoga student is encouraged to become aware of distortions, deceptions, and dishonesty in his thoughts and in his communications throughout each day. To better develop self-observation skills, he may also be asked to keep a diary and to note each day's experiences of being dishonest with himself or others. He may also be encouraged to anticipate the coming day's interactions in order to consider how he might put the principle of non-lying into practice. In following this practice, one first becomes aware of his more obvious deceptions. As he becomes more sensitive to the issue, gradually more and more subtle distortions in his thoughts and communications begin to surface and are corrected.

The practice of truthfulness is not intended to lead toward confrontational or aggressive behavior, for it is balanced by another principle: non-injury. Non-lying helps one to become aware of self-deception and of the way that one deceives others to gain an advantage. The practice of non-lying may also lead one to confront an underlying insecurity and an inner feeling of nonacceptance that motivates him to practice deception. He can then begin to face and deal with those feelings more directly rather than attempting to cover them up. The practice of non-lying also helps one to realize how he forms conflicting polarities through his deceptions, creating opposition between different aspects of himself and also between himself and others. With continued practice, the person experiences an ever-increasing sense of integration; his felt sense of opposition and conflict gradually dissipates. In this way non-lying (and each of the other nine principles) leads one from a feeling of divisiveness to a recognition of the underlying unity of being.

The following excerpts provide an example of a client in yoga therapy working with the principle of non-lying over the course of three therapy sessions.

First session:

C: *My friend and I met for lunch just before he was about to go on a trip. I didn't tell him what was on my mind. I was playing a role and I didn't realize it, although I was very aware that it was a real shallow get-together. I was denying the fact that I depended on him. I told myself that it didn't matter that he was going away for a while, totally denying the fact that I would miss him. I also told myself that I shouldn't feel sad. I think denial is what leads me to eat so much. I cover over my feelings and it leaves me with an uncomfortable sensation in my stomach. I use food to deal with that.*

T: *What could you have done instead?*

C: *Told him how I was feeling, that I was going to miss him, admitting, "I don't know how I'll deal with this loneliness while you're gone." But my attitude was real cocky: "Don't worry, I'll take care of myself." I was pretending it wasn't happening; I made myself numb. Overeating helps numb everything, helps suppress that feeling in my stomach. And once I start denying feelings, I create an unreal world. I made sure that I wouldn't miss him and get lonely. It even affected me when he came back. How could I have any good feelings on his return if I'd been denying all the time he was gone that I missed him? There were all these feelings that I was denying and being dishonest about.*

Second session:

C: *Over the weekend, I decided to do some writing about honesty. I became aware that if I had something to eat between meals, I wouldn't tell my friend. If I had two apples, I would lie and say that I had only one. If I had three colas, I would tell him I had two. I found that I want to control the situation by saying something that the other person wants to hear. I also found that being totally honest frees me up from trying to control anything except me. It makes me responsible for my own feelings. When I give excuses rather than the real reason for something, I start playing with how people are going to react to what I say, and it just snowballs. I saw how dishonesty was creeping into other areas of my life, and it didn't feel good. I saw that I had been wanting to make myself appear a little better than I was, not totally admitting where I was.*

T: *Did your behavior change after you wrote about this?*

C: *I'm more aware when I say something dishonest. I've stopped being dishonest about food and find I'm able to deal with my food intake. If I had a heavier breakfast or lunch this week, I was able to deal with exactly what I had and figure out what I was to have for dinner and still feel good about it.*

*I was surprised at how dishonesty was creeping into different parts of my life; for example, in not giving the real reason why I was late for an appointment. This morning was a perfect example. I was late for an appointment. I had trouble getting my car started, but even if my car had started right away, I still had gotten a late start. When I had trouble with my car, the first thing that went through my head was: I can tell him this is why I'm late.*

*It was really funny because I immediately recognized that that is the kind of behavior I want to change. It didn't make me feel good. So when I got there, I said, "I wasn't very motivated this morning. I was slow and that's why I'm late." I became aware that I was still reacting slowly, and we ended up laughing about it. That was an isolated situation, but a lot of little isolated incidents make me end up feeling not so good about myself, and those are the things that I found myself writing about. By committing myself to writing down my experiences, I set aside some time to myself. Even when I didn't write, I thought about what I was going to write.*

T: *Would it be useful to take ten minutes every night and review the events of the day to become more aware of how honest or deceitful you were?*

C: *Sure, it would be good to commit myself to writing ten minutes every night. That might keep me from avoiding some issues.*

Third session:

C: *I'm more aware of how uncomfortable I feel when I'm not honest with someone. I had something to deliver. It was supposed to come from the supplier by midmorning, so I made arrangements to deliver it at noon. But the supplier didn't show up until five o'clock in the afternoon, and when the guy finally came, he brought the wrong thing. I really wanted to run away. It is so hard for me to call my client and be upfront and just say, "We have a problem, and this is it." In the past, I would have made up some excuse. Instead, this time I simply told my client what had happened. Many little incidents like this have happened in the past few weeks. In the past, I avoided them or made excuses for them without even realizing it. Every time these incidents come up now, I feel: Here is another chance for you to practice being level with a person.*

*I have been thinking a lot about energy. It is as though I have a jar full of energy for the day. I can spend it negatively or positively. Every time I do something, I let a little bit of it out and by the end of the day, I want to see if it went toward productive things rather than worrying or making up excuses.*

The practice of non-lying does not give one the right to act aggressively toward another. As the following client is beginning to realize, non-lying and non-injury actually work hand in glove:

I've been trying to be more honest. Before, being honest meant trying to tell other people how I feel, but how I feel is usually based on my emotional reaction. A lot of times that hurts other people and it hurts me because my emotional reaction is not necessarily what is true about the situation. I've been real nearsighted in that sense. For example, my husband did something that made me angry. In the past, I would get totally wrapped up in expressing what I felt at the moment and I'd forget that two hours before, he'd done something really considerate. My whole attitude about what's honest is turning upside down right now. I'm trying to be a little more farsighted and objective when I'm in a tense mood.

To further understand the way the ten basic principles or commitments of yoga work to transform one's behavior and understanding of himself, let us consider an example from the second group of five qualities, those that deal with inner attitudes. One of those qualities is *santosha*, or contentment. As is true with all the principles, contentment helps to heal the fundamental split within oneself and between oneself and the external world. Contentment is the highest of all wealth. If a person has a million dollars and is not content, he is poor; if he has little means and yet is content, he is wealthy. In the modern world, many people live in a chronic state of discontent, experiencing a gap between where they are and where they would like to be. Most of their time and effort is spent in trying to change their circumstances, in striving to be someplace else. Yoga psychology encourages a contrasting or complementary attitude that relieves the chronic sense of dissatisfaction and engenders harmony both within and without. The following interchange illustrates the application of the principle of contentment to a person who had been expressing chronic dissatisfaction with herself. It also illustrates how yoga therapy can help one gain insight into the paradoxical nature of the phenomenal universe.

C: *I overlook the ninety percent good I do and dwell on the ten percent that I consider bad. I always think that if I would have done something a little differently, it would have turned out better.*

T: *One of the yogic principles, you know, is contentment. Have you ever worked with that principle?*

C: *No, contentment is one of those things I can't grasp. It is hard for me to imagine. I feel that I make mistakes in my decisions a lot.*

T: *Is it possible for you to feel that nothing you do is a mistake?*

C: *I don't understand. Do you mean is it possible for me to believe that whatever I do, I do for a reason?*

T: *It has a purpose.*

C: *But there still is such a thing as a mistake, isn't there? Are you trying to tell me that there's no such thing?*

T: *I'm wondering if there is such a thing. In your psychology there is the idea that there is such a thing as a mistake, but in reality I don't know.*

C: *That's an interesting thought. When you say that, I see a little light: viewing things as mistakes is being judgmental. I just don't want all this tension about having to change. If I put a concentrated effort into changing, I can't seem to do it.*

T: *There is nothing to achieve; that is what contentment means. If you are trying to make something be different, you are not content.*

C: *So if you are content, things in yourself don't need to be changed? You just accept yourself as you are? It's like giving up all criticism. And I suppose, I shouldn't put contentment out there as a goal either, and criticize myself when I'm not content.*

T: *I don't know if you should. You can put it out there as a goal, but it's not contentment if you do. You can't get to it as a goal, because contentment is already where you are.*

C: *If contentment is already where you are, why is it so hard?*

T: *Because you keep setting up those false goals, those ideals: "This is the way it must be done."*

Contentment, like many other qualities characteristic of unitary consciousness, cannot be reached by striving toward a goal, but can be realized only by letting go and experiencing where one is at the moment. Contentment does not lead to complacency, however, as many people imagine. The principle of contentment creates an inner sense of calm and peace, but it does not prevent one from working outwardly to bring about change. In working with the principle of contentment, one becomes increasingly aware that there is an ongoing growth process that makes change inevitable. He learns to be in harmony with the current situation even while he is bringing about change; he becomes increasingly peaceful and undisturbed by so-called failure or success. This dual attitude of being content and yet being in harmony with the process of change replaces the chronic restlessness, dissatisfaction, and stagnation so characteristic of many people's lives. The cultivation of contentment leads one from emotionality and from a preoccupation with narrow and petty concerns, which do not allow one to envision the many paths leading to his goal, to a sense of greater calm and openness. Paradoxically, the more one is content, the more he is open to change.

When one is content, it frequently has nothing to do with his objective circumstances. Discontent is an inner attitude that often would remain even if the person were to change his situation. The discontented person is not necessarily seeking change. He may be assuming a posture that actually makes change difficult. Yoga therapy helps such a person to relax his posture, to begin to accept his situation and open himself to possibilities of growth that he had not considered when he assumed his posture of dissatisfaction. Yoga therapy leads one to playfully explore alternative ways of acting and reacting in the world.

Many modern psychologists believe that if a person is content, his motivation dies. They believe that one must be restless and ill at ease to be creative and productive. But yoga psychology sharply distinguishes between contentment and satisfaction. Contentment refers to one's expectations. If one is not content with the fruits of his actions, he will be miserable. But one may be content with the results of his actions without remaining satisfied. Nonsatisfaction helps one to make efforts, without in any way preventing him from being content with the results of those efforts.

Instead of avoiding difficult situations, the student of yoga comes to view all situations as learning experiences, turning problems into opportunities for growth. A good example is provided by the woman quoted previously who felt she often made mistakes in her decisions. As she progressed in therapy, she found her attitude toward her job undergoing a change:

C: *All these little exercises that you have given me really help me enjoy my job a lot more. The other day, I had a choice of where to work in the restaurant, and I picked the place where I would have the most confrontation. My girlfriend asked, "What's wrong with you?" Everybody avoids that area because for some reason that is where anyone who would give you a hard time ends up sitting. I said, "Well, I figure it's an opportunity." She said, "I don't know what is going on with you." Afterward I thought about how much time I spend worrying that I might have to work there and trying to avoid it. There must have been some kind of change of attitude for me to pick that section to work in. And as it turned out, that section was really easy and it was waitresses in other sections who ended up complaining about problem customers.*

T: *Are you saying that it's your attitude that creates the situations you face?*

C: *I see that a lot. The waitresses who are looking for a hard time always get it. I have seen it work so fast. I don't know what it is about a waitress's body language or the look on her face, but somebody will give her the hardest time about something. Sometimes I tell her that I'll go talk to him, and he's really nice to me. You can see how people create their own environment. And when I got over my fear of certain situations, I stopped creating those situations to deal with.*

# Chapter Three

# THE RELATIONSHIP BETWEEN THERAPIST AND CLIENT

## RESPONSIBILITY

IT IS IMPORTANT TO EVALUATE WHERE the responsibility lies for making a person well. In modern medicine, the physician is considered to be the expert in fixing the body when it breaks down. His role is analogous to that of a mechanic fixing an engine, although of course the human body is far more intricate than any engine. There is little the patient can do but rely on the doctor's expertise and passively receive the treatment administered. The patient is expected to surrender his judgment to the expertise of the physician. This attitude toward treatment has carried over into the treatment of mental and emotional symptoms in what has come to be known as the medical model in psychiatry. It is not uncommon for the patient to enter therapy with the attitude that the therapist is an expert who will administer a treatment that will cure him while the patient himself remains relatively passive. Of course, this model of therapy fits in with some of the patient's needs and fantasies. The patient may prefer to avoid facing certain conflicts and weaknesses in himself and thus escape the considerable effort involved in changing. The appropriateness of generalizing from the medical model and applying it to problems of living has been called into serious question,[1] and certainly there are many psychotherapists who are not in agreement with it. However, the medical model continues to be prevalent in much of modern psychiatry.

In addition to standard medical treatments, there are other physical treatments that encourage a relatively passive attitude on the part of the client and emphasize the expert's responsibility in bringing about a cure. These approaches may have a marked temporary effect, but if the client does not learn to take continuing responsibility for his functioning and to change previous habits, the symptoms that led him to seek treatment are likely to reappear. Such passive treatments occur in the psychological sphere as well. Hypnosis is perhaps the most obvious example. It can produce marked changes in symptoms, but there has been a long-standing controversy over whether such changes are lasting, whether symptom substitution occurs, and whether a person who undergoes hypnosis is giving up responsibility for himself.

The movement from treating symptoms in isolation to dealing with the whole person leads to a change from the medical model, in which the expert takes responsibility for the patient, to the conception that the main work of the physician or psychotherapist is to teach the person how to take increasing responsibility for his own life. By concentrating on the suppression of isolated symptoms, the physician or psychotherapist can frequently create the illusion that in his bag of tricks he has the means to make the patient well. But when one recognizes the role of symptoms as signals of underlying disunity, the focus moves to the underlying discord itself. From this perspective, the work of the physician or therapist is to help clear the way for the client to alter his way of living and being in order to become unified within himself. The physician or therapist can assume the role of coach or teacher, but he cannot "fix" the patient, as is assumed in the medical model. He in fact encourages the client to take increasing responsibility for the various facets of his life.

Yoga is a holistic training program rather than a method

of treatment.[2] The yoga therapist does not treat patients; instead he may teach, coach, guide, or otherwise assist fellow players in the game of life. His method of teaching is not didactic but consists of an ongoing dialogue with the client. He may provide guidance, but it is up to the client to practice the techniques of self-transformation. The client gradually learns to take responsibility in each aspect of his life—physical, interpersonal, mental, emotional, and spiritual.

The issue of responsibility is vitally important. Therapists have noted that the neurotic person does not take responsibility for his words and actions.

> The rifts in the neurotic's personality do not permit him to be "present" to the same degree in his actions and words as are healthier personalities....A comparatively healthy person will...retain the feeling that he made a decision....A severely neurotic person...will be inclined...*to feel:* I have no choice.
> ...neurotics feel, "I did it, but I did not want to do it." Or, "I wanted to do it, but at the same time I did not want to do it."....
> ...such a patient does not feel at one with his own words and actions....It is the analyst's task to make the patient feel responsible for his own words and his own actions....
> ...*making the patient feel responsible for his own words* is equal to *curing the patient.*[3]

Typically, the client entering psychotherapy feels at the mercy of outside forces; he does not feel that he is freely choosing his way of being. This is reflected by the words he uses. The client denies responsibility in using such expressions as "I have to" or "He made me." The client will say, "He made me angry" or "He hurt my feelings." The yoga therapist may respond to such a statement by asking whether the client could have chosen any other response than anger or hurt. Gradually, the client learns that he chooses to respond in a particular way.

"Shoulds" and "have tos" also play a large part in the lives of many clients. One client reported:

> When I was growing up, my mother would give me the feeling that to take any option other than the one she wanted me to take would be bad. Her attitude was, "This *should* be done right now in *this* way." If I did it any other way I'd be doing it the wrong way. Now I have a sense of guilt if I don't do things I feel are expected.

When a client says "I should" or "I have to," he is expressing his unwillingness to stand behind his actions and accept full responsibility for them. To the yoga therapist, such expressions are jarring and make no sense, because they imply an inherent disunity within the personality. The therapist may challenge the perspective on which they are based and offer another in its place. The interchange between client and yoga therapist may go something like this:

C: *Doesn't everyone live with "shoulds?"*

T: *I'm not sure. I wonder what it would be like to live without them for a day.*

C: *But then I wouldn't have any controls over myself. I might do anything.*

T: *Gee, that sounds exciting! I wonder if you'd be willing to try and live without "shoulds" and "have tos" for a few hours one day this week.*

One client was told she *should* never do what someone tells her she *should* do. This paradoxical injunction helped to free her from the "tyranny of shoulds" which is experienced by so many neurotic patients.

As therapy progresses, the client begins to replace "I have to" with "I choose to." He learns to take responsibility, to become integrated or whole rather than split by conflict between "what I want" and "what I am supposed to do." He also comes to understand that it is counterproductive to impose "shoulds" on others, for it often leads to a response that is the antithesis of what is sought. A client who had been in therapy for some time and had been working on this issue described the following interchange with her daughter:

C: *This morning I told my daughter that she should wear her boots today. "Should" just automatically came out. She said, "I don't want to wear my boots today." I told her that there was snow on the ground. She said, "I don't like boots." Then I thought about how we've talked here in therapy about the feeling that we "should" do something. So I said, "Actually, I guess you really don't have to, but if you don't, your feet will get wet." She said, "I like my feet to get wet." I told her, "I don't like my feet to be wet. I like to wear my boots, but if you don't mind your feet being wet, then I guess you don't need to wear your boots." She said, "Okay." She started out the door without them and then she came back in, saying she had decided to wear her boots, and she put them on.*

*We are just so inundated with these "shoulds," like, "Your room should be neat." It took me a long time to give up that one. Right now at this point in my life, I feel that there is nothing more important than allowing my children to know what their own feelings are rather than telling them that they should or should not behave in a certain way. I can point out possible consequences of what they do, but I also acknowledge that they may not care about those consequences in the same way that I do. If they are not burdened with a "should," they can do something and learn from it. Then they won't have this big hangup that they did the wrong thing. If my daughter catches a cold from going without her boots, it doesn't seem like a big thing.*

T: *Do your children respond differently since you've adopted this way of relating to them?*

C: *Yes, I think so. One day my daughter said, "That is just your opinion" to a friend of hers. It gives them a certain amount of freedom, and they can tell me what they think or feel. It works out good in my family to say, "It's just your opinion," and it's not the Almighty Word that is being passed along. They can disagree with it. I might make them do it my way anyway, but at least they are free to know they don't always have to do it my way or think the way I do.*

The emphasis on self-responsibility in yoga therapy extends to the therapist as well. While a physician who follows the medical model assumes responsibility for curing the patient, he may take little responsibility for his own physical, psychological, or spiritual well-being. In the same way that a mechanic's ulcers or obesity have little effect on his ability to fix an engine, in the medical model the physician's well-being or lack of it is considered to be irrelevant to his ability to operate on his patients or to prescribe for them. He need simply apply the techniques he has learned. He may give "sound medical advice" about diet, smoking, exercise, and so on, whether he himself follows the advice or not. This contrasts with yoga therapy, where the principle "Physician, heal thyself" is of primary importance. Jung was in agreement with this perspective. He unequivocally asserted that

> analytical psychology requires the counter-application to the doctor himself of whatever system is believed in— and moreover with the same relentlessness, consistency, and perseverance with which the doctor applies it to the patient.
> ...The demand...that the doctor must change himself if he is to become capable of changing his patient, is...a rather unpopular one...because it is sometimes exceedingly painful to live up to everything one expects of one's patient.[4]

## The Role of Modeling

While imitation as a means of learning is given little importance in modern psychology, in other cultures modeling has been regarded as an extremely important mode of learning. For example, the *Ramayana*, an ancient epic of India, gives little in the way of direct instruction. Rather it teaches through the examples of the characters in the epic. In describing Rama, the hero of the epic, the *Ramayana* tells us: "Whatever he did he ennobled by the way he did it." Rama and his wife, Sita, were exemplars for the entire society to emulate. The *Bhagavad Gita* directly states that a good role model is essential. Krishna, the enlightened teacher who is free from all desire and the need to act on his own behalf, tells Arjuna, his disciple:

> *In the actions of the best men others find their rule of action. The path that a great man follows becomes a guide to the world.*
>
> *I have no work to do in all the worlds. . . . I have nothing to obtain, because I have all. And yet I work.*
>
> *If I were not bound to action, men would follow my path of inaction. If ever my work had an end, . . . confusion would reign. . . .*[5]

In yoga therapy, the relationship between the teacher and the student takes precedence over the teaching of mechanical procedures, abstract content, and behavioral prescriptions. When content is taught, it is within the context of a relationship, and what is conveyed by the relationship is considered to be more important than the content. Likewise in yoga therapy, the presence and way of being of the therapist plays a greater role in influencing the client than the content of what the therapist says.

Some of the most enlightening examples of the way in which teaching occurs through imitation and of the power that ensues when verbal instructions are congruent with the expression of one's entire being are found in the life of Mahatma Gandhi. Gandhi did not advocate anything that he did not practice himself; he always experimented on himself and found what the results would be before he taught anything to another person. The story is told that one day a mother brought her child to Gandhi and informed him that the child was eating a great deal of sugar. She said to Gandhi, "Please tell my child that sugar is harmful and that he should stop eating it. He won't listen to anyone else, but he respects you so much that he will listen to you." Gandhi thought for a moment and said, "Bring your child back in two weeks and I will talk to him." The mother and child lived far away and the mother was annoyed that they would have to make the long trip a second time. But she wanted the child to stop eating sugar, so she agreed. When they returned two weeks later, Gandhi simply told the child that sugar is bad for one's health and that he should not eat it. The mother was grateful, but her annoyance grew. She asked, "Why did you have us come all this way again?" Gandhi replied, "Two weeks ago, I was still eating sugar."

## SELF-ACCEPTANCE

The approach of the yoga therapist in working with behavior change may be straightforward. The therapist may recommend that the client undertake specific practices that lead to more functional behavior. But many clients do not respond to this direct approach. Although they may say they are highly motivated to change, they fail to practice new routines on a regular basis, if at all.

A client's thwarting of the goals of therapy, his reluctance, unwillingness, or inability to follow the therapist's guidelines or prescriptions, is labeled "resistance" by many psychotherapists. In physics, the term "resistance" refers to a force that tends to oppose or retard motion. Freud adopted this concept and applied it to what he believed is the ego's opposition to the recall of unpleasant experiences. Subsequently, the use of this term broadened. The term is now used to indicate that the client is resisting the process of change: "Resistance may vary from rejection of counseling and overt antagonism, on the one hand, to subtle forms, such as hesitation and inattention, on the other. Clients may say: 'I know what I want to say, but I can't say it'; 'I'll have to leave early today since I want to study for a test'; 'I don't think that applies in my case'; 'I'm sorry I'm late, but I almost forgot about our interviews'; 'I thought you were supposed to be the expert.'"[6] The use of the term "resistance" reflects the egocentric perspective of the therapist who has, singly or with the client, defined a goal and views the client as not carrying out his part in attaining that goal. The client's behavior is considered to be defensive.

From a less egocentric perspective, however, one might say that it is the therapist who is resisting the client, for the therapist is neglecting to consider that the client may not actually be failing to progress toward the client's real goal. The client's goal may simply be different from what was stated verbally, agreed upon, or expected by the therapist. The therapist is not taking into full account all that lies behind the client's agreement to carry out a task and his subsequent unwillingness or seeming inability or failure to do so. From this perspective, resistance is a two-person game that the therapist helps to create. The payoff is that the therapist can blame the client for not changing, while the client concludes that the therapist must be incompetent, since the therapist is not bringing about an alleviation of his symptoms. If the client's goal is to defeat the therapist, he may be quite successful.

Seen in a more positive way, it may be important to the client to establish his independence and autonomy by failing to carry out prescribed behavior. If the therapist looks behind the verbal contract to the unspoken interchange, he is likely to discover that these are initially quite at odds with one another, and that they merge only when the therapeutic process has succeeded. If the therapist tunes into, deciphers, and responds to the unspoken dialogue and to the client's frame of reference, he may view the client's behavior not as resistance to growth, but an expression of his attempt to grow. From this perspective, the client is never resisting; he is always in the process of growth. If the therapist helps the client become aware of the way in which his attitude or behavior is part of the growth process, he can avoid the stalemates that often occur by labeling behavior as resistance. The client enters therapy complaining of symptoms or qualities within himself that he would like to eliminate. The yoga therapist, however, may help the client to experience their positive value. For attempting to eliminate a quality perpetuates it, whereas recognizing its value helps one to become less preoccupied with or fixed upon that quality and allows him to move on.

What is labeled resistance is actually the externalization of an inner conflict that the client experiences between two aspects of himself. One part of the client makes a demand, and another part asserts itself against the demand. It is important that the therapist not become aligned with either side, that he maintain a neutral position with regard to all polarizations within the client. If the therapist feels that the client is resisting him, it is because the therapist has aligned himself with one side of a polarity. Resistance is an illusion. Demands necessarily create resistance. Resistance dissolves to the extent that demands are given up.

As long as the client focuses on what he defines as unacceptable feelings, thoughts, and actions, and attempts to eradicate them, he creates a tug-of-war within himself between the "good" or judgmental part of himself that demands change and the part that is resisting being eliminated. The energy on each side of the polarity is equally matched, so neither side can ultimately win. One side may temporarily overcome the other, as when an obese client refrains from eating sweets for a week. But the temporarily subdued side will sooner or later gain its revenge; the contrary part will eventually reassert itself and become dominant: the client will one day call his therapist to tell him that he has just eaten four chocolate bars and a large piece of cake. A therapist who identifies with one side of the client's internal battle will inevitably be disappointed. The therapist may become dejected as a result of his imagined failure, or he may take out his frustration on the client.

Paradoxical interventions can be extremely valuable in helping the client and therapist out of these deadlocks. While such interventions, which involve the encouragement of symptomatic behavior, have found increasing use in modern psychotherapy, they are not a new discovery. They have long been used in spiritual traditions to lead students out of the stalemates they create for themselves. The following anecdote from the life of Rabbi Wolfe of Zbaraj from the Hasidic tradition exemplifies "the acceptance of symptomatic behavior, with a view toward the creation of a context where change is possible."[7]

> People came to him to denounce some Jews who were playing cards late into the night.
> "And you want me to condemn them?" he cried out. "Why me? And in the name of what? And for what crime? They stay up late? It's a good thing to resist sleep! They concentrate on the game. That is good too! Sooner or later they will give up card-playing—what will remain is a discipline of body and mind. And this time they will place it in the service of God! Why then should I condemn them?"[8]

This story illustrates the way in which "the therapeutic paradox accepts the symptomatic behavior, but creates a context within which it can be put to more productive ends. It draws on the client's...strengths, so that when the problem-supporting context is transcended, these strengths remain to be utilized in the service of growth."[9]

In Zen Buddhism, paradox is used in a different way. In

the Zen tradition the spiritual guide may use a koan to encourage the student to exaggerate symptomatic behavior—in this case, his rationalistic reasoning process—until the student becomes so frustrated that he experiences a breakdown in that framework, and a new mode of consciousness emerges. The koan is

> a mental exercise whose absurdity or paradoxical nature blocks the faculty of rational comprehension and thereby makes it fail. What then enters into consciousness is an awareness of one's world image precisely as an *image* of reality and not reality *itself*. Indeed, there is reason to assume that the so-called mystical experience occurs when...we manage to leave...our world image and for a fleeting moment succeed in seeing it "from the outside" and thus in its relativity.[10]

Aikido and other Eastern martial arts use a similar principle. In these arts, instead of opposing the force of an attack with a counterforce, one uses the energy and momentum of one's opponent, turning the opponent's own force against him. One may accentuate the thrust of the opponent's attack and thereby help it to complete itself in a way that defeats its antagonistic purpose. One continues to turn the aggressor's thrusts back against the aggressor until the attacker surrenders, defeated by his own efforts.

In psychology, if the therapist creates expectations or opposes the client's "resistance," the client and therapist may become locked into a tug-of-war. But if instead the therapist aligns himself with the antagonistic or "resistive" client, the client's position as antagonist becomes untenable. If the client wishes to continue as an opponent to the therapist who is encouraging "resistance," he must adopt a new position—one that is identified with growth. Or the client may give up the game and arrive at a more spontaneous way of relating and being, which is not based on one-upmanship. In either case, the client must change.

The therapist, for instance, may find that the client will not carry out behavioral prescriptions. Instead, the client attempts to set up a power struggle in which the therapist is supposed to get the client to change or improve, while the client's role is to maintain his symptoms or get worse. In such a situation the yoga therapist may direct the client to increase his symptomatic behavior. In one case, an anorexic client was given weekly prescriptions for behavior change, but they were not directly related to eating. This was done in order to determine how she would respond to directions. The client would return each week and report that she had been unable to follow through on the instructions. The therapist then told her that she was too heavy, and agreed with her that food is repulsive and that she should not force herself to eat. He suggested that she go on a fast and lose a minimum of one pound in each successive week. He continued to express his disappointment as the client returned each week to report a slight increase in weight.

The yoga therapist may join in the client's perspective and up the ante. At a superficial level it may seem that he is not taking the client seriously, that he is discounting or mocking the client, but actually it is the client's ploy or the limiting role with which the client identifies that the therapist does not take seriously. The therapist's unwillingness to be involved in the transaction that the client is attempting to set up may lead to more intimate and genuine sharing between client and therapist.

One client who consistently did not follow his therapist's prescriptions enjoyed giving lengthy and detailed descriptions of his inability to overcome his problems. The therapist then made a show of beginning to record their sessions, telling the client that he was writing a book on failures in psychotherapy and that the client was an excellent case upon which to base his book. Furthermore, whenever the client began complaining about his lack of success, the therapist would indicate for the tape recorder that this was a section of the therapy session to be transcribed for his book. As the client's complaints diminished and he instead began to describe positive changes in his life, the therapist began to complain that all the time and effort he had spent in collecting material for his book had been wasted. After a time, the client improved considerably and began giving credit for his improvement to all of the people who he said had helped him. The therapist then complained that he expected to receive all the credit and that furthermore he expected the client to go around telling everyone else how much he had been helped by the therapist. The client soon began asserting that he himself was responsible for his own behavior, and not others.

The yoga therapist may express the client's negativity or doubt in an accentuated or exaggerated way, or he may encourage the client to exaggerate or advertise his plight to others. One client reported that he felt burdened with obligations, as though he were always carrying a heavy weight on his shoulders. He expected the therapist to make suggestions about how he might be relieved of his burden, but instead the therapist encouraged him to accept and pay greater attention to his experience, even to make it worse. The following interchange took place:

C: *I let the load build unconsciously without feeling it at all for a while, and then gradually I just begin to feel worse and worse without realizing why. Finally, I feel so miserable that I say, "All right, what's the matter?" or I'll be rude or feel like I want to withdraw.*

T: *I had a crazy notion of you getting some canned food and taking the labels off and then relabeling them with your burdens, like "taking care of the dog," "getting my papers done for school," and so on. Then you can put the tin cans into a sack and carry them on your back. Your sense of being burdened and the burdens themselves would be more obvious to you. You could really feel the weight of those burdens.*

C: *Everyone would know then.*

T: *Not necessarily. The cans would be inside the sack, so people would just know you're carrying something.*

C: *I could set them out in front of me and just stare at them, or I could measure the weight; I'd know if they were growing.*

T: *Yes, you could actually add or subtract weight as your burdens change.*

C: *It would drive home the point. I guess I could keep in the backseat of my car a box of canned, prepackaged, unspecified burdens of various sizes—one-pound, two-pound, three-pound cans—and I could label them as needed. Well, that would sure bring it home to me. It's such a senseless pattern. It's like carrying around a bag that I don't have to carry around simply because I got out of the awareness of carrying it. I forget I'm carrying it around.*

The yoga therapist may lead the client to side with the unwanted part of himself, and he may also encourage the client to side with another person who is antagonistic to the client. Clients often describe problematic relationships with parents or with others who they find demeaning and disrespectful. Some clients have sought love and acceptance from a parent for years on end, but each contact brings simply another rebuke, to which the client responds by feeling dejected, inadequate, or angry. This pattern is repeated again and again. The client envisions no alternatives except to try once more to win his parent's love. In such situations the yoga therapist may help the client to respond to the parent much in the same way that an aikido master deals with someone who is trying to be an adversary. If a woman is criticized by her mother each time they speak on the phone, the therapist may suggest that she anticipate her mother's criticism and side with her. The daughter may be instructed to begin the conversation by criticizing herself. In this way she steals the mother's thunder. She takes control of her mother's anticipated thrust and completes it in a way that is not painful to herself. Furthermore, since the daughter is now occupying her mother's position, her mother has little choice but to give her daughter the support that she had been seeking all along.

In dealing with inner conflicts, the therapist may encourage the client to accept and appreciate both sides rather than identifying with one and rejecting the other. One client who had been so encouraged reviewed her recent therapy sessions in the following words:

> A month ago, we talked about my ambivalence about money. You suggested that I approach it by setting aside one or two days a week for dealing extensively with money—paying my bills, studying about investments, and so on—and another day or two a week for avoiding money completely. I realized that my tendency was to try to force myself to choose between two opposite inclinations rather than making room for both. I had a flash of intuition: I perceived that behind your suggestion was the idea of respect—respect for all the different sides of myself.
>
> I tried to imagine what it might be like to exercise this kind of respect in my life, and the first thing that popped into my mind was sweets. My craving for sweets has always been one of the things I really dislike in myself, not only because it contributes to my being overweight, but also because it conflicts with my interest in good nutrition. And yet it always seemed that the more I resisted it, the more it tried to take me over. I wondered if it would be possible to respect the sweets craving and allow it expression rather than being at war with it. So I determined to try it out.
>
> For about two weeks, I ate good meals for breakfast and lunch. Then for dinner, I ate only sweets—as much as I wanted. It became a great game to find the most gooey, delicious, high-calorie extravaganzas available. Chocolate nut brownies with thick frosting became my favorite, so the game became find-

ing the best brownie in the city. Eventually, I began to crave good food with my sweets dinner. So I started eating protein and vegetables at dinner, and sweets didn't fight back. I began eating fewer sweets overall, but always made sure to set aside at least one time during the day that was sweets time. Right now, I am satisfied with a dish of ice cream after lunch, along with an occasional goodie at other times when the idea of sweets jumps up and demands attention. I don't spend nearly as much time and energy as I did before either thinking about what sweets to get or trying to resist the urge.

In order to allow the client this sort of freedom and acceptance, the therapist must remain a neutral witness, free from attachments to either side of the polarity with which the client is struggling at the moment. He may attempt to clarify the struggle that the client is putting himself through, but he remains a model of one who has disengaged from identification with polarities and their ensuing dramas.

If a client assumes that he has failed at something and then generalizes and labels himself a failure, he creates and will remain caught in a vicious cycle. Since he already sees himself as a failure, he will lack the self-confidence and enthusiasm to succeed, and so is bound to fail at any new venture. If the therapist encourages him to be a success, he will fail at that as well, and the therapist will inevitably experience disappointment. But the yoga therapist is likely to respond to such a client by defining him as successful no matter what he does. The yoga therapist helps the client to adopt this new perspective and thereby replace the negative cycle with a positive one. Ultimately he will lead the client beyond the polarity of success and failure.* From the monistic perspective, polarities are all considered to be illusory.

---

* If a client were identified with being successful, the yoga therapist would also challenge this limited identification, pointing out the ways in which this self-definition does not apply. His aim would be to lead the client beyond identification with either end of the polarity.

Resistance/compliance, success/failure, and so on are illusory conceptions that make no sense from the monistic point of view. How can one fail when every experience is part of the process of awakening to one's full nature? With this view, the yoga therapist may confront his client's illusions. Here is an example of such a confrontation:

C: *I'm afraid of failure.*

T: *What do you mean by failure?*

C: *I failed at my marriage.*

T: *I don't understand the word "failure"; that word doesn't make any sense to me. Haven't you learned anything from that relationship? Haven't you grown from it?*

C: *Well, I got a divorce.*

T: *Okay, but why do you call divorce a failure? You have a preconceived notion of the way it's supposed to be and when it doesn't turn out that way, you call it failure. Then you spend your time blaming yourself, feeling guilty, and programming yourself to feel incapable rather than productive. What if you didn't create that gap, but accepted yourself as you are? In my mind, there is no such thing as a failure. The way I see it, you grew to the extent that you were able to in that experience; you learned what you were ready to learn. It's true you didn't come close to an ideal relationship, but then you weren't ready for an ideal relationship. Rather than accepting where you were, your limitations and their consequences, you deny the reality. You have an ideal that you project onto yourself and the relationship, and then when you don't measure up to the ideal, you call yourself a failure. What an interesting plot! It would seem to me that you and your ex-wife are still each learning what you are capable of learning from each other, whether you are divorced or living together.*

From the perspective of unitary thought, what was viewed as problematic turns out not to be a problem at all, that is, the situation is viewed in a positive way.

As with a Chinese finger lock, the more one struggles, the more he becomes entrapped. Paradoxically, when one accepts himself, he becomes more fluid and begins to change. The way out of this client's conflict is not to struggle to become a success, but to accept all aspects of himself. The ultimate goal in this case is to transcend the polarized conception of success and failure.

Many people mistakenly think that the attainment of some goal will lead to self-acceptance and acceptance from others, but acceptance based on attainments is superficial and ultimately disappointing. One really wants to be accepted and loved unconditionally for what he is underneath the masks he wears. The search for acceptance underlies everything that one seeks in life. All the melodramas in which a person becomes entangled—such as those based on identification with success and failure and good and bad—involve a lack of acceptance by oneself and others.

To the extent that the therapist truly accepts himself, he is able to model self-acceptance and to accept his client. All psychotherapeutic methods are insignificant in comparison with the expression of unconditional acceptance. In fact, all interventions are primarily the means for the therapist to express or deny acceptance. To the extent that the therapist can express and the client can experience unconditional acceptance, growth and healing take place; to the extent that acceptance by the therapist is lacking, growth and healing are restricted.

The client comes to therapy disowning the parts of himself that he considers unacceptable. He believes that those unacceptable aspects of himself create his suffering, but it is actually his non-acceptance and disowning of aspects of himself that create all the melodramas and unhappiness in his life. When one accepts the unwanted parts of himself, they cease to dominate him. The yoga therapist, therefore, encourages the client to acknowledge all aspects of himself. The following client is beginning to see how helpful self-acceptance is.

C: *I'm trembling, and it's embarrassing.*

T: *I wonder what it would be like if you accepted the trembling as part of yourself, instead of trying to fight it.*

C: *You said that to me once before, about accepting emotions, when I feel intensely angry toward my daughter. At first when you said it, I thought, "Accept that? I can't accept that. That is a really despicable part of me." I've thought about it a whole lot since then and what a hard time I do have accepting aspects of myself that I don't like. I know that is what meditation is all about, letting go completely and not trying to be anything. It is so utterly simple and then at the same time it's so fantastic, so profound.*

Leading one to accept all parts of himself does not mean encouraging him to act them all out—in fact, acceptance has quite the opposite effect. When portions of oneself are not accepted, a melodrama ensues in which the unwanted part is given a leading role. The unconscious acts out the unwanted part or one projects it onto others while the conscious mind plays the complementary role. But when one befriends the unwanted aspect, both sides give up the charge that is created between them and sustained by their artificial separation and polarization. The energy that had been tied up in maintaining the polarity is then freed and the person experiences increased vitality, inner joy, and unity. Here is an example:

C: *All I've wanted to do all my life was to live up to my mother's expectations. I've always tried to be what she wanted me to be. But when I accomplished something my mother wanted, I didn't feel any different. For instance, I didn't feel any more worthy for being on the football team, and so I had to go and do something else. I wondered, What am I going to do next to get that feeling of being worthy? Then I would find a new activity. But I never felt worthy within myself. My worthiness always had to come from some accomplishment, and even then there wasn't a real sense of self-worth inside—just a very temporary feeling of having accomplished something outwardly. I've never really felt worthy, and so I've always been trying to do things to feel worthy.*

T: *What would it be like to accept being unworthy, to feel, I'm unworthy and that's okay. I don't have to become worthy.*

C: *[After a long pause] It's a relaxing thought. If I could just relax and say that it's okay. It's like the game is over; I can just sit back and relax. I can feel that! What a relief! That is a real pleasant thought. I don't have to say anything or defend myself or be better than you or be anything else.*

T: *You seem different.*

C: *I can just settle into that thought. It's like a reprieve. It feels so good. I wonder how long I could be unworthy.*

T: *How long?*

C: *Would it bother me? I'm looking at it like a vacation.*

T: *How about if you accept your unworthiness for a week and then reevaluate it? I wonder if you could feel unworthy and let the people around you know that you are unworthy.*

C: *I don't know how I could do that. I spend too much time showing them that I am worthy. How could I do that?*

T: *How about wearing a sign that says "I am unworthy."*

C: *Then I would have to explain to everyone why I'm so unworthy. The people at the office would think that I'm crazier than a loon, and that sign is the final proof. They would probably insist that I wasn't unworthy. I would say to them, "You think that I'm worthy, but I'm not. I've been feeling unworthy for years and now that I'm finally content with that feeling, you're trying to ruin it." That's very interesting. I might even get to feeling worthy. If I accept my unworthiness, there won't be anything to feel unworthy about, so I'll feel worthy.*

A week later, this client returned to say:

> What I was viewing as a flaw and a disturbing thing turned out to be something entirely different. The minute that I quit battling it and was willing to just let it be as it is, the most remarkable thing happened. My lifelong foe turns out to be my long-lost brother. I can throw off my armor and embrace it. It was a really remarkable and exuberant experience when its clothes came off and it wasn't what I thought it would look like at all.

In such ways the yoga therapist may use paradoxical interventions to help a client get in touch with and accept unwanted aspects of himself. He may instruct the client to accept, advertise, or increase the very behavior that the client wishes to eliminate. This type of intervention may loosen the hold that a particular polarity has over the client. Here is another example of such a strategy:

C: *No matter what I accomplish, there is still that image down deep of being second-class, and I don't know how to get rid of it.*

T: *I wonder if the first step might be to accept it. You say that you've been trying to hide it.*

C: *Accept it? I don't want to be second-class.*

T: *Perhaps you could become more aware of how you feel second-class in various situations. Maybe each day you could deliberately do something that is second-class. Let someone know that you are second-class and then study that.*

C: *What?*

T: *How about eating the leftovers?*

C: *I usually do eat after everyone else, and I get the leftovers.*

T: *You could consciously do one extra thing every day that you consider second-class.*

C: *Any other suggestions?*

T: *Maybe there is even third-class. You might explore being third-class.*

The yoga therapist encourages the client to befriend the unwanted aspects of himself and to recognize the useful function that they serve. Whereas the medical model focuses on the suppression of symptoms, in yoga therapy one's suffering is the open door that can lead to significant growth. It is the signal that something is wrong and a clue to the source of the disturbance. If the signal is successfully suppressed, the growth process will be delayed until the signal erupts again, perhaps with greater force or in another aspect of one's physical or mental functioning.

If one's doorbell rings, he usually answers the door: he does not cut the wires to stop the bell from ringing. However, in dealing with signals from within, many people try to interrupt the signal, so the message that something is wrong does not get through. For example, if a person has a headache, he takes aspirin so that the pain that is signaling that he needs to slow down, or that he has eaten overly rich foods, or that he has

made himself tense and worried, no longer reaches consciousness. As a result, he never deals with or corrects the
underlying disturbance. Perhaps other symptoms will appear,
such as shakiness or heartburn. If those are also repeatedly
treated with symptom-suppressive drugs, the underlying problem will finally express itself in the form of a more dramatic
signal, such as a heart attack, which leaves increased structural
damage. Now the message "Change your lifestyle, the way you
deal with your body, your work, your relationships" gets
through for a short while, until the palliative effects of pharmaceutical agents again establish a false sense of reassurance,
and one falls back into the old habits.

By contrast, if one works with a yoga therapist, he will be
encouraged early on to pay greater attention to his suffering
rather than avoiding it, to become aware of the situations and
inner attitudes that bring on the suffering, and to change
those aspects of himself that lead to suffering. From a yogic
perspective, all suffering is regarded as having a positive, valuable function. When faced directly, pain and suffering can be
seen as the greatest of blessings. Paying attention to pain and
tracing it to its source makes one aware of areas of existence
that need to be attended to. One grows little from outward
success, for a person falsely clings to success as a source of
security, and as a result becomes stagnant. On the other hand,
suffering, when acknowledged and traced to its source, creates
the greatest opportunity for growth. The presence of pain
motivates one to correct imbalances within himself and in his
relationship to his environment.

This is not to say, of course, that it is necessary or advis-
able to seek out suffering. Clearly, a prime goal in life and the
purpose of all therapy and of yoga is to eliminate suffering. But
this cannot be achieved through suppression or denial and
subsequent displacement. Suffering can be eliminated only by
becoming fully aware of what the pain is signaling. The message that pain bears is often so surprising or startling to our
limited ego-consciousness that we have extreme difficulty

comprehending where the message originates and what it is actually saying, and so we do not know how to respond to the distress we are experiencing. Only by truly understanding the nature and source of suffering, and acting on that understanding, can we eliminate suffering from our lives.

Frequently it is our petty ego, our unnecessarily delimited self-definition, that is the source of pain. Our ego's refusal to accept certain aspects of experience causes us to feel that we are suffering. By changing our attitude, by viewing things in a different light, by accepting the world as it is, we eliminate our distress. For ultimately it is not life that needs to be changed, it is only our attitude. A situation or experience that we have been viewing solely as a source of misery can, by a change of attitude, come to be seen as something positive and good. The following two case histories help to illustrate this principle.

The first involves a middle-aged man who was a professional violinist and who had had his arm crushed by an automobile that struck him as he was crossing the street. He was depressed and embittered when he consulted the therapist a few months later. He could not understand why such a fate would befall him. During the first interview, the therapist asked him whether anything positive might result from the accident. The client questioned how the therapist could entertain such an absurd notion. As the sessions continued, the therapist occasionally introduced similar questions about the positive changes that might come about as a result of the injury. The client gradually began to comment on the leisure time he now had to pursue neglected interests, in contrast to the hectic pace of his life before the accident. As therapy progressed, he began to recognize that his life had been stagnant for a number of years. He had long fantasized about moving to a warmer climate and beginning a new line of work, and he recognized that now he was in a better position to make those changes. He began taking exploratory trips to the South and made plans to settle there. Six months after the start of therapy, he acknowledged that despite the pain and suffering it had caused him, the accident had led to significant growth in his life, and indeed was one of the best things that had happened to him in years.

The second client was a lawyer who began therapy just after he had been fired for embezzling money from his firm. He sobbed during the therapy hour as he described his fear that his career was ruined. Getting caught embezzling seemed to him to be the worst thing that could ever happen to him. During the first few weeks of therapy he explored his motivations for embezzling and reported that ever since he was a teenager he had wanted recognition from his father, who was a highly successful businessman. Each time he had accomplished something, he had turned to his father for acknowledgment, but his father always found fault with what his son did. The son thought that if he showed his father how successful he was by having an expensive house and car and other costly possessions, he would finally win his father's approval.

This client began to realize how much significance he was giving to his father's opinion of him in many aspects of his life, even in choosing a mate. In further sessions he began to explore other avenues for experiencing that he was lovable and competent. Gradually he began to divest his father of the power and authority he had been giving him. He came to recognize that being caught embezzling was a turning point in his life, for had he not been caught he would have gone on living with the same desperation. But being fired freed him from repeatedly seeking his father's approval. He even began to recognize ways in which he had made it quite easy for others to discover his theft, as though he had deliberately designed the course of events as a way out of his predicament.

These two situations illustrate how a situation or experience that is initially regarded as negative can be turned into a positive force in one's life by understanding its value and the potential it has for helping one to grow. Yoga psychology takes this perspective in regard to any situation, no matter how awful it may initially seem. Each situation is an opportunity for one to make great strides in his growth toward improved interaction, transcendence of ego-identification, and a more comprehensive consciousness.

## THE EXPERIENTIAL BASIS OF YOGA THERAPY

The client in therapy ordinarily identifies with the thoughts and feelings he experiences during the therapy hour; he becomes swept up in the dramas that his thoughts and emotions create. He takes himself all too seriously, losing all sense of playfulness and joy. He may wallow in complaints, disappointments, fears, or self-deprecation. The yoga therapist is a neutral witness to the postures of the client and the melodramas in which the client is entangled. He encourages the client to disengage from the melodramas and to give up his posturing, so that together they can discover what lies behind the role and the character that the client is assuming.

The client expects the therapist to take his melodramas seriously. When instead the yoga therapist remains lighthearted or amplifies and exaggerates the client's predicament, the client may complain that the therapist is making fun of him. The yoga therapist may acknowledge that, in fact, he does not take as very real or exciting the client's attempt to gain sympathy and his feigning ineptness, confusion, or victimization. There is something beneath all the client's acts, however, that he does take very seriously. He is waiting patiently to share at a more intimate level than is possible when the client remains identified with a particular role.

At times the therapist may be more than a witness. He may choose to be playful, to cajole, or to share his own fantasies and craziness. The therapist thereby helps the client to value the client's own "craziness." The following dialogue between a therapist and a client who was himself a graduate student in psychology illustrates the way in which the yoga therapist may playfully challenge the client's assumptions.

This may initially frustrate the client who is trying to make the world fit his assumptions, but eventually such dialogues may lead the client to break out of his limited perspective and become more spontaneous and alive.

C: *The first session was my gripe session and this is my second session. Let's get into prescriptions. Let's spend this session more directed so that I can walk out of here and feel some kind of direction that is different or unique. I want to know what you can do for me.*

T: *I think that the question is: What can you do for you?*

C: *Okay, fine, I see that, but can you tell me some things about myself? In lectures you talk about chakras and energies and things like that. Can you make some interpretations of my behavior or personality makeup?*

T: *How would that help you?*

C: *I'd then have more of an understanding about myself; I would know what I need to work on.*

T: *It seems you know a lot conceptually already.*

C: *I guess I need to confirm my suspicions about myself. You don't give at all. You answer questions with questions, and you do a good job of getting me frustrated.*

T: *Do you feel frustrated?*

C: *I went to this other therapist and he made an interpretation about my problems and the flow of energy in my body.*

T: *How did that help you?*

C: *I can keep my mind focused on my personality structure and on* what I do and how I do it in terms of my personality type.

T: *What type do you want to be? If you had a diagnostic label, you wouldn't have to be yourself. You could say, "What can I do? I'm this particular way, and that's simply the way I am."*

C: *Then I would deal with my limitations more.*

T: *Exactly. That's what I'm saying. But maybe you don't have limitations.*

C: *I don't?*

T: *Just the ones that you impose upon yourself in your fantasies.*

C: *So how do I change? What will change me? How will I change myself?*

T: *How do you want to change yourself?*

C: *I want to hear you talk, to feel like I'm getting my money's worth.*

T: *I already gave you more than your money's worth.*

C: *Why do you say that?*

T: *Your money isn't worth that much. It's not worth as much as you are.*

C: *How much am I worth?*

T: *What do you think?*

C: *I don't know. I guess that is what I am trying to discover. Well, if I were a therapist, I would have something in mind for my patient; I would have some general precept for what was going on.*

T: *Maybe I'm just trying to drive you crazy. Maybe that's all there is to it.*

At times the therapist may be playful; at other times, he may assume a more serious attitude toward the client, but he does not become identified with the role of helper or teacher or adopt a pose of solemnity. If a client says the opposite of what he means, it is sometimes necessary for the therapist to do the same, so that they can get together and realize that they understand and accept one another. Some of the most meaningful moments in therapy occur when client and therapist are able to share their craziness.

The heart of yoga therapy consists of a Socratic-like dialogue, a meeting between two human beings. The yoga therapist has oriented his life around the monistic perspective, while the client is operating from a different model of the universe. The client's assumptions lead him to experience addictions, aversions, and conflicts within and between himself and others, as well as emotional turmoil, insecurity, and lack of clarity about the meaning and purpose of his life.

The yoga therapist does not base his response upon theories or methods he has learned secondhand from books; rather, he uses his own experience gained in dealing with and overcoming suffering in his own life. He does not try to impart his experience by didactic teaching; instead, he opens himself to take in and respond to the experiences of the client. In this process the client will sometimes describe experiences that are foreign to the therapist, not because the therapist is unfamiliar with those experiences, but because they grow out of an entirely different set of assumptions than those from which the therapist functions. The therapist seeks to comprehend what the client is saying in terms of his (the therapist's) model, but finds that it just does not fit. As a result, he may stop the client in mid-sentence, confronting him with his duplicity. For example, a client will typically describe his behavior with such expressions as "I should," "I have to," "I can't," and "I'll try."

These words reflect an inner split between one part of him that is making a demand and another part that is reacting to the demand. This reaction may take the form of compliance, resistance, feigned compliance, panic, fear, immobility, or some other response.

Concepts like "I should," "I have to," and so on are not part of the worldview of a therapist functioning from a monistic perspective. They make absolutely no sense to him, so he lets the client know this. He encourages the client to explain what he means by such verbalizations, for they do not exist in any dictionary written from the therapist's perspective. The therapist may say to the client, "What do you mean by saying 'I'll try'? That seems dishonest. To me, trying implies merely making a show of effort. It is a posture of non-success. Is trying something that you do in order to remain as you are?"

On the other hand, the yoga therapist remains open to the client's phenomenology rather than automatically interpreting the client's experience according to a preordained framework. He is willing to let go of any preconceptions, including those formulated in this book, in the face of the client's experience. While fully acknowledging the client's experience, the therapist also remains sensitive to and accepting of his own experience. The therapist does not allow himself to become identified with the client's scenario and to take the role that the client has scripted for him. The yoga therapist may confront the client if he experiences attempts by the client to confuse, mislead, or distract him, or if he experiences a diminution in spontaneity or directness in their relationship. The therapist's challenges to a client are based not so much on conception as on his own experience. Though he may verbalize his experience within a conceptual framework, his experience of himself and the client is primary.

Therapists like to go to workshops to learn methods and techniques, but these are actually superfluous in psychotherapy. If one is living from the perspective of the dualistic or monistic paradigm, all techniques will inevitably evolve out of the assumptions of that paradigm and out of the therapist's experiences. He need not learn methods developed by another therapist.

To the extent that the therapist is genuinely self-accepting, he will provide an environment in which the client can discover self-acceptance. Techniques often camouflage and create diversions to hide the therapist's lack of self-acceptance. The self-accepting therapist is more likely to respond with spontaneity and innovation in his encounter with a client, forging a unique intervention that is suited to the moment rather than rummaging through an old bag of tricks.

The client typically enters therapy with certain assumptions about himself and his life. These may include:

1. Someone or something else is responsible for my condition and circumstances.
2. Somewhere out there in the world is what I need to be happy.
3. I want something different from what I am getting.
4. The predicament I am in is very important, serious, and real.
5. I *have* to do certain things, and I *should not* do other things.

To the yoga therapist, these assumptions are not valid. They are based on a frame of reference and logic that is foreign to him. It is as if the client were saying, "I walk on my head in the sky." The therapist tries to make sense out of what the client is saying. He asks, "What do you mean by that?" He may offer his own alternative assumptions to the client, not as truths to be believed, but as a different set of working hypotheses with which the client can experiment. Especially in the beginning, the assumptions of the therapist functioning from the non-dual paradigm may well be antithetical to those of the client. The assumptions of the non-dual therapist include:

1. I am fully responsible for my own condition and circumstances.
2. What I need to be happy is already here within myself.
3. I am getting exactly what I want, and when I begin wanting something different, I will get that.

4. Any predicament I seem to be in is self-created in order for me to learn to let go of addictions. If I let go, I will find that my perceived predicament is not so serious, important, or real, and I will begin to treat it in a playful way, which will open up all sorts of positive possibilities for responding to it.
5. I *choose* to do certain things. I *choose not* to do certain other things.

As the relationship develops, the client has the opportunity to encounter the assumptions of the therapist, to apply them to himself, and to observe their effects. The yoga therapist is not a guru or a fully enlightened being. He is merely another person seeking freedom from suffering and awareness of his true self. He offers what he has learned and invites the client to experiment with new attitudes toward himself and others.

The relationship is far from one-sided. The therapist who is open to what the client is experiencing may learn from the client as much as or more than the client learns from the therapist. Perhaps the client will also challenge the therapist's limiting assumptions. At times the client's model may be more conflict-free than that of the therapist. A client may present a way of experiencing that calls attention to the therapist's insensitivity or lack of awareness and points out an area in which the therapist has yet to grow. The yoga therapist opens himself to the client's wisdom and uses the meeting as a growing experience for himself. Clients may teach the therapist about compassion, fortitude, humility, serenity, and any number of other qualities that may not be well developed in the therapist. The therapist may often wonder who is teaching whom. He may hear words of wisdom and see expressions of admirable qualities that provide examples that help him grow. Even the less admirable qualities that the client expresses can make the therapist aware of the many facets of himself. The therapist often finds that the process of helping the client to deal effectively with his problems is also helping the therapist to deal effectively with his own.

# Chapter Four

# THE COLLECTIVE UNCONSCIOUS
# FROM THE YOGIC PERSPECTIVE

## CHAKRAS AND ARCHETYPES

IN HELPING A PERSON TO BRING unconscious contents and modes of experience into awareness, yoga therapy includes but goes beyond the personal unconscious. It works extensively with a deeper layer of the unconscious, where universal archetypal themes have their play. This layer of the psyche, which Jung called the collective unconscious, plays a far greater role in motivating a person than does the personal unconscious.

Tantric philosophy and psychology offers a comprehensive model for understanding the archetypal themes around which human life revolves. This model refers to specific centers, each of which creates a unique mode of experience. These centers are called chakras. The English words "circle" and "circus" are derived from the Sanskrit word "chakra." A circus is a circular arena with tiers of seats in which public entertainment takes place. Similarly, each chakra is an area in which a particular form of entertainment or drama occurs. Typically, one is involved in the drama, but if one develops his powers of self-observation, it is possible to become a spectator of the grand show that occurs at each chakra. The word "circus" also refers to a circular area where many streets intersect. In the same way, each chakra is a center at which many forces intersect in a human being. Each chakra may be likened to the hub of a wheel, with spokes radiating outward from the center. The forces that radiate out from each chakra affect one's physical, emotional, and psychical functioning.[1]

Jung pointed out that

the chakras are symbols. They symbolize highly complex psychic facts which at the present moment we could not possibly express except in images. The chakras are therefore of great value to us because they represent a real effort to give a symbolic theory of the psyche....

...we are studying not just consciousness, but the totality of the psyche. The chakras...become a valuable guide for us in this obscure field....

They are intuitions about the psyche as a whole, about its various conditions and possibilities.[2]

In the system of chakras, the archetypes that are considered primary are organized into an evolutionary hierarchy, ranging from those that are predominant in more primitive modes of experience to those that come to the fore only in the more highly developed modes of consciousness. The manner in which consciousness evolves through the archetypal modes of experience is reflected in both phylogenetic and ontogenetic development and in the structure and organization of the human organism. According to tantra, there are seven primary modes of consciousness, each quite distinct from the others. Each mode of consciousness has a corresponding physical center. The most primitive form of consciousness is related to energy and physical processes that take place at the root of the spinal cord. As consciousness evolves, it is localized in progressively higher centers along the spinal cord and brain, culminating in the seventh chakra at the crown of the head (see figure 1). Jung noted that "the chakras of the Tantric system correspond by and large to the regions where consciousness was earlier localized, *anahata* corresponding to the breast region, *manipura* to the abdominal region, *svadhisthana* to the bladder region, and *vishuddha* to the larynx and the speech-consciousness of modern man."[3]

There is a well-known story about a man who finds himself standing in front of two closed doors. Behind one door is a beautiful lady and behind the other, a tiger. The experience awaiting him behind one door is dramatically different from the experience awaiting him behind the other.

## The Chakras

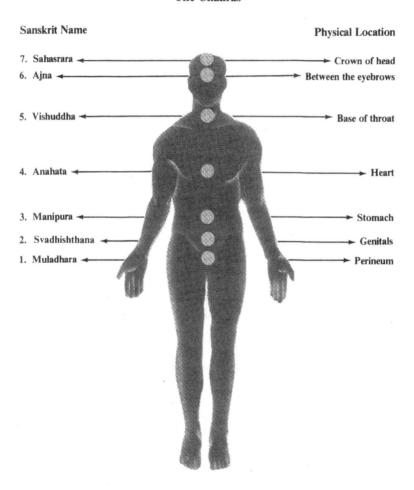

| Sanskrit Name | Physical Location |
|---|---|
| 7. Sahasrara | Crown of head |
| 6. Ajna | Between the eyebrows |
| 5. Vishuddha | Base of throat |
| 4. Anahata | Heart |
| 3. Manipura | Stomach |
| 2. Svadhishthana | Genitals |
| 1. Muladhara | Perineum |

Figure 1

Now imagine that a person is standing before seven closed doors. However, instead of the doors being all on one level, they are arranged one above the other, with a spiral staircase connecting the different levels. If the person were to open any one of the doors and enter the environment within, his experiences, his way of thinking, his emotional states, and his way of relating to others would be entirely different from what they would be were he to ascend or descend the staircase and cross the threshold of any other doorway. This is analogous to the different modes of consciousness of the seven chakras.

A similar metaphor is employed by the Pueblo Indians:

> There is a Pueblo myth according to which man was gener-
> ated far down in the earth in a pitch black cave. After untold
> ages of dormant and absolutely dark wormlike existence, two
> heavenly messengers came down to them and planted all the
> plants. And finally a sort of cane grew up, which was jointed
> like a ladder and long enough to go through the opening in the
> roof, and so mankind could climb up and reach the floor of the
> next cave; but it was still dark. Then after a long time they
> climbed up in the same way and reached the third cave. And
> then again, ages later, they climbed up to the fourth cave, and
> there they reached light, but an incomplete and ghostly light.
> That cave opened out upon the surface of the earth; but it was
> still dark. At last they learned to make a brilliant light, out of
> which the sun and the moon were finally made.
> You see this myth depicts very beautifully how conscious-
> ness came to pass, how it rose from level to level. Those are
> chakras, new worlds of consciousness of natural growth, one
> above the other.[4]

As Jung noted, "each chakra is a whole world."[5] Each is a different realm of one's internal environment with its own decor, textures, mood, and atmosphere creating a unique mode of experience. Within that setting, there are particular story lines and interactions. The dramatizations of each chakra consist of a dance around a particular polarization and are based on an attempt to come to terms with a basic polarity in the world of names and forms, for each polarization creates an interaction, and the chakra is the focus of that interaction. At each chakra a primary archetype is expressed in the form of a dramatic representation. Each chakra has its unique scenario involving a protagonist, a foil, and supporting characters. These parts have been enacted from time immemorial in myths, fairy tales, recorded history, and the theatrics of everyday life.

In disturbed functioning, one becomes mired down and continues to repeat the same lines and the same scene again and again. Psychotherapy is a means for freeing a person from his fixation upon particular lines so that the drama can complete itself and reach a resolution. When one is under the spell of an archetypal realm, he becomes identified with and loses himself in the roles created by that archetype. Resolution occurs when he becomes aware that the polarities created by the enactment are insubstantial and he ceases to identify with the dramatization, becoming free from his entanglement in that mode of experience.

At each chakra, the same archetypal drama is enacted time and again by countless people in various times, places, and costumes. Although there may seem to be an endless variety of enactments, they are actually variations on a single theme. The apparent differences are the result of changes in setting and costume rather than changes in the basic plot. In the same way that motion pictures may stage the conflict between good and evil as a Western, a modern-day big-city police story, a futuristic science fiction drama, a pirate adventure, or any number of other possible forms, so the playing out of an archetypal drama may be clothed in various garbs and embellished with a large variety of subplots. Superficially the drama changes with every enactment, but the essence is ever the same.

## TABLE 1
## Chakras and Archetypal Themes

| Chakra | Mode of Experience | Ideal Representation(s) | Polarities Experienced | Examples |
|---|---|---|---|---|
| 7—Sahasrara | Unitary consciousness | No representations; beyond form | none | Shankara, Meister Eckhart, Shiva in meditation |
| 6—Ajna | Insight, witnessing | The sage | sage/fool<br>objective observer/deluded participant | Socrates, Lao-tsu, Immanuel Kant, the Wizard of Oz, the Delphic Oracle, Merlin |
| 5—Vishuddha | Devotion, receiving nurturance and unconditional love, surrender, trust, creativity, grace, majesty, romance | The child | object of devotion/devotee<br>mother/child<br>found/lost<br>trust/distrust | Christ Child with Madonna, St. Teresa of Avila, Hanuman, Sri Ramakrishna, Don Quixote |
| 4—Anahata | Compassion, generosity, selfless loving, service | The mother<br>The savior | rescuer/rescued<br>liberator/liberated | Blessed Virgin Mary, Jesus, Mother Teresa of Calcutta, Albert Schweitzer, Gandhi, St. Francis |
| 3—Manipura | Mastery, domination, conquest, competition, inadequacy, inferiority, pride | The hero | gain/loss<br>success/failure<br>dominance/submission<br>blame/praise | Alexander, Napoleon, Hamlet, Prometheus, Superman, all sports and military heroes, corporate presidents, political leaders |
| 2—Svadhishthana | Sensory pleasure | The hedonist | pleasure/pain<br>male/female | Bacchus, Eros, King Henry VIII, Ravana, Salome |
| 1—Muladhara | Struggle for survival | The victim | predator/prey<br>life/death | Movie monsters and their victims, Hitler and the Jews of the Holocaust, The Inquisition, Hansel and Gretel and the Witch |

Table 1 presents a synopsis of the archetypal themes that are enacted at each chakra. The table may be thought of as an evolutionary ladder. At the bottom is the most primitive mode of consciousness and at the top is the most evolved.

Each archetype exists within each person, along with all the characters and enactments that unfold from each archetype. However, most people are especially involved with a particular chakra and a specific part. They may at times enact parts in dramas from other chakras, but they return again and again to the role that dominates them, whatever that may be: rebellious child, mother, seductress, second best, outsider, hero, coward—any of the innumerable roles that exist in human life. Those parts that one does not consciously adopt remain in the unconscious and are also projected out onto the world, where they are observed secondhand.

The archetypal themes that are acted out are impersonal and universal, but a person usually identifies with the part he is embodying and thinks that he is acting as an individual. He thinks of himself as actually being the character he has assumed; he does not realize that the role he plays on the world stage is not his true identity. An important goal of psychotherapy is to have the person cease to identify with the part and the drama that he has taken as his own. Jung warned that

> you must not identify with the unconscious. You must keep outside, detached, and observe objectively what happens . . .
> The idea of an impersonal, psychical experience is very strange to us, and it is exceedingly difficult to accept, because we are so imbued with the fact that our unconscious is our own—my unconscious, his unconscious, her unconscious— and our prejudice is so strong, that we have the greatest trouble to dis-identify.* [6]

---

* Jung's view that there is a single universal or collective unconscious that is being expressed through many people may appear to be similar to the conception in Vedanta psychology that there is only one consciousness. But for Jung, the universal unconsciousness stands in juxtaposition to the individual ego, which is the center of consciousness. By contrast, Vedanta psychology asserts that the universal consciousness alone exists.

The various forms of psychotherapy are aimed at freeing human beings from their identifications with particular enactments and from the limitations, distress, and suffering that result when one identifies with any part or dramatization. However, psychotherapy typically leads a person to free himself from one part in an archetypal drama only to replace it with another. For example, one may gradually cease identifying with the role of the incompetent bungler and instead begin acting in a self-confident manner. This substitution of a new part that enjoys greater rewards seems to be a means of leaving behind the limitations of the less desirable part. However, new limitations, conflicts, and distress will soon be experienced in the new part as well. One continues to remain in the same drama despite the switching of roles.

## BEYOND SUBLIMATION

The way a person can transcend the conflicts engendered by his absorption in a particular chakra is to stop identifying with that realm entirely and to become absorbed in a chakra further along on the evolutionary ladder. Then the polarities and conflicts that were so absorbing will be left behind. By evolving to a higher chakra, one achieves a new worldview, and the old conflicts are transcended. From the perspective of the higher chakra, the former conflicts will be seen as illusory distinctions with no real significance. One will experience new polarizations, but these will be more subtle. As one moves up the ladder of evolution, the polarizations encountered become increasingly less conflictual and less absolute. There is a progressive decrease in the experience of opposition and an increasing awareness of the complementary and supportive nature of polar qualities, culminating at the most evolved chakra with the realization that all polarities are the illusory manifestation of unitary consciousness.

The view that energy may be transformed and expressed

in less conflictual ways is also found in modern depth psychology. According to Freud, the more primitive modes of experience are primary, but primitive drives can be channeled or sublimated into more constructive modes of expression. This conception of sublimation reflects Freud's reductionist bias. Jung, on the other hand, did not regard any instinct to be primary. He believed that psychic energy finds a number of different channels of expression; it can be expressed through any archetypal model with no mode being inherently more fundamental than any other:

> For Jung the concept of *libido* has a different or rather a wider meaning than it had for Freud. It comprehends the sum total of the energetic life processes, of all the vital forces of which sexuality represents only one area. Jung speaks of libido as an energy value which is able to communicate itself to any field of activity whatsoever, be it power, hunger, hatred, sexuality, or religion, without ever being itself a specific instinct. In other words, the psychic functioning is understood as taking place within a number of relatively autonomous areas each of which is invested with a certain amount of energy.[7]

Jung himself offered the following metaphor:

> In physics... we speak of energy and its various manifestations, such as electricity, light, heat, etc. The situation in psychology is precisely the same. Here, too, we are dealing primarily with energy, that ... can appear in various guises. If we conceive of libido as energy, we can take a comprehensive and unified view. Qualitative questions as to the nature of the libido—whether it be sexuality, power, hunger, or something else—recede into the background ... I see man's drives ... as various manifestations of energic processes and thus as forces analogous to heat, light, etc. Just as it would not occur to the modern physicist to derive all forces from, shall we say, heat alone, so the psychologist should be beware of lumping all instincts under the concept of sexuality. This was Freud's initial error, which he later corrected by his assumption of "ego-instincts."[8]

From this perspective, "all religions as well as cultural expressions become an authentic point of psychic existence and cannot be regarded as derivative. Hence the concept of sublimation becomes void. In its place we find the concept of *transformation*."[9] Transformation, in contrast to sublimation, implies that no particular mode of psychic energy is primary, but that one mode can be changed into another.

Freud viewed the developmental process from the perspective of one who looks upward from the lower rungs of a ladder. He believed that the lower rungs formed the foundation but that one could climb upward from this starting point. In Jung's metaphor of the transformation of energy, primacy is not given to any mode of energy expression. Monistic psychology takes a third position that appears to be the complement of Freud's view: it looks at the evolutionary process from the top of the ladder. As Jung noted, the chakras "symbolize the psyche from a cosmic standpoint. It is as if a super-consciousness, an all-embracing divine consciousness surveyed the psyche from above."[10] In the monistic view, the unitary mode of experience is primary and expresses itself in progressively more gross and materialistic forms as it descends through the chakras. From this perspective, evolution does not consist of sublimating the basic energy, but of progressively freeing consciousness from its entanglement in the illusory forms manifest by each of the chakras, beginning with the most primitive. Only when one is identified with a particular archetype does that mode of consciousness seem to be primary.* When one moves to a more evolved mode of consciousness, the perspective changes, and what had seemed to be important and real becomes insubstantial and unimportant. The conception that a conflict can be resolved by embracing the perspective of a more evolved chakra has a parallel in modern psychology in the conception of second-order

---

* It is because of such identification that Freud gave preeminence to the sexual drive and that subsequent theorists emphasized other archetypal modes of experience.

change, which involves, as previously noted, "a quantum jump...to a different level of functioning."[11]

Yoga leads one to leave his absorption in one chakra and to reach a higher perspective, and then to leave the new perspective behind for a still more evolved mode of consciousness. One passes through a series of evolutionary changes. Each time he awakens from one dream, he finds himself enmeshed in a more subtle dream. This process continues until he reaches unitary consciousness.

## SURVIVAL

In the most primitive mode of consciousness on the evolutionary scale, an animal or human being remains absorbed in coping with life-threatening situations. In order to survive, he preys upon other life forms and avoids being preyed upon himself. This preoccupation with survival is found most dramatically in animal life, in some primitive societies, and in uncivilized conditions where law and order has not been established or has broken down, such as in the "Old West," in war, prison life, and street gangs. This mode of consciousness is also predominant in large-scale or private catastrophes, such as floods, tornadoes, serious automobile accidents, and medical emergencies. But the experience of this archetype is not reserved for primitive or catastrophic situations: concern with survival is part of the fabric of modern life. If one glances at the headlines of a daily newspaper or watches the evening news on television, he is repeatedly reminded of the nuclear arms race, armed conflicts, disease, automobile and airplane accidents, mass unemployment, economic concerns, and brutal muggings and murders. One carries with him an ongoing concern about his safety and his ability to survive.

As if those concerns weren't enough, we also seek out fictional dramatizations in which threats to survival are central. Some of the most popular motion pictures focus on this theme. There are countless medical, disaster, war, and crime movies in which one vicariously experiences the struggle for survival. Many motion pictures vividly portray the brutal murder of one human being by another. Horror movies abound in which primitive, powerful, animal-like creatures maim and murder innocent victims. The popularity of such movies indicates the degree to which human beings are haunted by the fear that a primitive, uncontrolled savage beast within or without will rise up and destroy them. Perhaps watching such movies and emerging from the theater unharmed provides one with a sense of mastery over the threats to his life. Many people also seek out situations that are or appear to be dangerous in order to assure themselves of their invulnerability. Race-car driving, hang gliding, or going on thrill rides at an amusement park are examples of such experiences.

The mode of consciousness in which one is preoccupied with survival is experienced in the *muladhara* chakra, the lowermost chakra, located at the base of the spine. *Muladhara* is a Sanskrit word meaning "root support." This chakra is related to solid matter, or earth: "In muladhara ... we are rooted in the soil."[12] Here one has a materialistic perspective; he identifies with his physical existence. A young man who was serving a prison term for rape provides an example of the worldview of a person living within the compass of this archetype:

> I like to live with animals. That is how I base my life. People don't realize it, but I stalk them like an animal to see how they react. An animal stalks and sees what the prey will do. If the prey runs, then the animal goes after it. He kills to survive; I fight to survive. No matter what, I'll survive.

One role in this dramatization is that of the aggressor— the murderer, rapist, predator. The reciprocal role is that of the potential victim who fears being attacked. Below, two women in psychotherapy who are absorbed in this role describe their experiences:

Cl: When I was a young child, I remember having terrible fears. I couldn't go down from the second floor to the first floor without my father at one door and my friend at the other. My back would be against the wall, and I'd be running, panic-stricken all the way. I was terrified of the dark. I did get locked in the basement once. Now I won't shut a door, let alone lock it. I was terrified of death. If I saw anything on TV about death, I was horrified. I've had a terrible fear of being raped, even though I've never even come close to it.

C2: When I got home from group last week, my husband hadn't left the porch light on, and I was really scared. I ran into the house. I'm afraid of dying a violent death, of being tortured to death. I read the other day where this woman was coming home from a job, and three men picked her up and raped her. I have a fear of that happening to me. There are so many things that do happen, people being killed or raped. That's all you see in the paper. If I hear a noise in the house, maybe it's just a creak or something, I start imagining that somebody is trying to get in. I lock my bedroom door when I'm alone, and if there was a fire, I don't think that I would ever get out because I have so many locks.

Such themes often appear in psychotherapy sessions.

In yoga therapy, there are various means of helping a person transcend his identification with a particular part in an archetypal dramatization. The yoga therapist helps the client to see the drama that is being enacted in a more comprehensive context. This may be accomplished by leading the client toward awareness of how the theme that preoccupies him has been enacted in other settings and with many variations. The client may be encouraged to read stories, myths, or other descriptions of the archetypal drama and to understand it as an archetypal enactment. He may also be encouraged to alter the script. For example, he may be directed to exaggerate his part, making it more extreme; to seek out additional opportunities to play the part he is already playing; or to experiment with different roles and outcomes.

A person with a phobia may be instructed to purposely exaggerate his fear or to experiment to determine whether he can intentionally create the situation he fears. For instance, a claustrophobic client was afraid of being trapped in a subway train after it lost its power or in an elevator stuck between floors. Whenever he rode the subway or stepped into an elevator, he would become preoccupied with thoughts that the car might stop at any moment. This client was asked if he believed in "mind over matter," if he thought it might be possible to will the car to stop. When he agreed that this might be possible, he was asked to carry out an experiment each day that week when he rode the subway. He was instructed to will the car to stop with his thoughts, for no more than ten seconds. As he carried out this prescription, his uncontrolled panic reaction was replaced by new responses that were under his conscious direction. His fear diminished. Another client was afraid of fainting on the street. She was encouraged to pretend to faint and also to make herself faint on purpose, with a similarly beneficial result. Of course, this paradoxical approach of encouraging symptomatic behavior and bringing it under the conscious control of the client is not unique to yoga therapy. But when this approach is used in yoga therapy, it is done in the larger context of helping the client to understand the purpose and value of his symptomatic behavior.

Such paradoxical prescriptions often lead the client to see the humor in his scenario, to take his part less seriously, and to realize that it can be modified. In some cases, the client who is identifying with the victim role may be encouraged to take the reciprocal role—to imagine that he is the perpetrator or predator—and to experience the world from that perspective. This helps the client get in touch with the complement of his usual role, to become aware of the polarization he is creating, to transcend his identification with one part, and to reach reconciliation between the reciprocal roles. An even more effective means of helping one out of the fear and paranoia created when he enacts this archetypal theme is to lead him to the perspective of a chakra further up in the evolutionary hierarchy. From that new perspective, the creak in the house or the stranger one encounters will not inevitably be experienced as a cause for alarm.

In the first chakra, polarization is most extreme: one's opposite is experienced as a threat to his very existence. At the next chakra, one's opposite is experienced as both threatening and alluring; here one seeks one's opposite instead of running from it or trying to eliminate it. At the third chakra, one's opposite is seen in a competitive light. As one progresses further up the ladder of evolution, he increasingly experiences the two sides of a polarity as supportive and complementary, finally reaching the zenith of the evolutionary journey, in which the two poles are experienced as illusory manifestations of one unity. The system of chakras traces the transition from reductive to dualistic to monistic modes of experience (see table 2, p. 90). Indeed the paradigms result from the experiences of specific chakras. Each of the various psychological models takes the perspective of a particular chakra and explains the human being from that perspective.

## PLEASURE

When one enters the realm of the second chakra, svadhisthana, he leaves the concern with survival behind. At this chakra, one is dominated by the pleasure principle: he desires to attain and maintain pleasurable experiences through all sensory channels and to avoid unpleasant experiences. He may be consumed by his desire for sensory or erotic pleasure. Considering physical sensation to be primary, he lives a materialistic and hedonistic life. He identifies with his physical body and fears growing old or dying and losing his capacity for sensory experience.

## TABLE 2
## Chakras and Psychological Models

| Chakra | Mode of Experience | Psychological Theorists or Models |
|---|---|---|
| 7—Sahasrara | Unitary consciousness | Advaita Vedanta |
| 6—Ajna | Insight, witnessing | Yoga, Buddhist psychology |
| 5—Vishuddha | Devotion, receiving nurturance and unconditional love, surrender, trust, creativity, grace, majesty, romance | Jung |
| 4—Anahata | Compassion, generosity, selfless loving, service | Rogers, Fromm |
| 3—Manipura | Mastery, domination, conquest, competition, inadequacy, inferiority, pride | Adler, Ego psychology |
| 2—Svadhishthana | Sensory pleasure | Psychoanalysis, Reich, Bioenergetics |
| 1—Muladhara | Struggle for survival | Primal scream therapy |

Believing that the sources of pleasure are to be found outside himself, a person operating from this center seeks a sexually attractive partner, delicious foods, stimulants, physical comforts, or any other object or experience that he imagines will give him sensory pleasure. He is ruled by desire for the objects that give him sensate pleasure, and spends most of his time and energy pursuing such objects. All other goals become secondary. When under the sway of this hedonistic mind-set, one may be willing to sacrifice security, prestige, friendship, acceptance by society, and perhaps even his very life in order to attain pleasure.

In his pursuit of the objects of pleasure, one experiences considerable unrest. The chase often ends in frustration or disappointment. Even if one attains his goal, he may find that the experience of pleasure is insufficient and fleeting. For instance, after his sumptuous meal is finished, he will begin searching for another pleasurable experience. He will become addicted to those objects that give him pleasure and will frantically attempt to re-create experiences that have given him pleasure in the past. When he is not able to recapture a pleasurable experience, he will become frustrated and angry, and if someone else attains the object of his desire, he will experience jealousy. The pursuit of pleasure gives rise to a number of scenarios that are repeatedly portrayed in soap operas and in real life.

Today in our society, many people lead a life in which they are preoccupied with the pursuit of pleasures of various sorts. They spend their free time indulging the senses through eating, drinking, sexual activities, the use of drugs, and other means of attaining sensory gratification. Some experience a sense of emptiness or incompleteness in this pursuit. Others are torn by conflict between the pursuit of pleasure and needs that arise from other archetypal modes of experience. Here is a woman who is experiencing just such a conflict:

> Yesterday I got up at 6:00 a.m. and meditated and did hatha yoga. I ate well, and later in the day I jogged. Today I'm smoking two packs of cigarettes and I'll probably go to a bar and get drunk. I love to smoke and drink together. There's something about having cigarettes and drinking that's real nice. But it's not what I want to do. I can feel what it's doing to my body.
>
> There are two distinct parts of me: the part that would love to sit in a monastery, and the part that could do a lot of drugs and go to bars every night and pick up men. If I do everything I want to do for three or four days, the next day I'll feel even more like going to the opposite extreme. Somebody told me

once, "You can't be a whore and a nun at the same time. Make up your mind." Well, I can say that I want to be the whore and it's real fun—all this drinking, partying, and stuff—but it's not satisfying to me. There's always that part of me that's saying, "This is not taking you to a place you want to go."

I've slept with so many guys and smoked lots of dope. I've had my share of booze and partying, and that doesn't make me happy. There's no lasting value to me doing all that stuff, any more than indulging in an ice-cream cone; it's good for just while you're doing it. But if you tell people that you don't smoke, you don't do drugs, and you can't stay up late because you want to get up early in the morning to meditate, they don't understand. They think you're very weird.

Just as there are many people who are preoccupied with the pursuit of pleasure, so conversely there are many people who believe that pleasurable sensations are wicked and that they should not allow themselves to experience sensory pleasure. Although they may have intense desires for sensory gratification, they place severe constraints on themselves. But repressing one's desire for pleasure only gives it increased power and significance. If this mode of experience is not allowed expression, a hysterical disorder or some other form of psychopathology is likely to occur. Such reactions were prevalent in the Victorian era and prompted Freud to focus on the pleasure principle as the chief motivating force in human beings. Freud analyzed human experience and behavior in terms of the second-chakra mode of experience. For Freud, the pleasure principle was primary; all other motivations and modes of experience were seen as secondary elaborations of the urge to experience pleasure.

Wilhelm Reich and Alexander Lowen also view human existence from the perspective of the second chakra. Their psychologies emphasize the capacity to experience sensory pleasure as the measure of a human being's fulfillment. They emphasize the positive aspects of this mode of experience and assert that a human being should fully experience his capacity for orgasm. Their therapies focus on removing muscular and characterological blocks and inhibitions in order to increase one's experience of pleasure. The methods they use can help one achieve that end, but their therapies neglect to look beyond the pleasure principle to recognize the significance of other realms of experience.

According to yoga psychology, the loosening of blocks to this mode of experience is an intermediate goal. Once one has realized his capacity for pleasure and also the limitations of this mode of being, he will be ready to turn his attention to still other realms of experience. While the second chakra brings one pleasure, it does not lead to lasting satisfaction but only to temporary appeasement. During periods in which sensory stimulation occurs, one experiences pleasure, but at other times he experiences unrest, frustration, and other unpleasant states. The desire for pleasurable experience is like a fire that can never be quenched. The more one feeds the flame of desire with the fuel of objects that gratify the senses, the more intense the flame of desire becomes. The more one enjoys, the greater becomes his desire for continued and more intense enjoyment. If one experiences repeated enjoyment, he eventually tires of that experience and seeks out variations that will engender new pleasures. His desire makes him restless; it leads him onward to seek new sensory experiences. In this mode of experience, one ordinarily feels a lack within himself and searches outside for that which he believes will give him pleasure. Only when he finds that object and incorporates it into himself does he temporarily experience pleasure.

In trying to attain pleasure, one creates tension within himself that actually diminishes his experience of pleasure. The most intense sensory pleasure actually occurs when one gives up all pursuit and relaxes his entire body. For most people, that relaxation occurs only after having attained the sought-after object. But if one learns to relax and experience his own organism rather than pursuing something outside himself, he will find that the experience of pleasure is inherent in that relaxed state. Then he will experience that intense sensory pleasure that is already a part of one's being and is not dependent upon uniting with an external object. Reich was aware of this. In his therapy, he emphasized the relaxation of chronically tense muscles and the capacity to experience intense sensory pleasure throughout one's body, independent of external objects.

In yoga therapy, one may learn techniques that lead him to very deep states of relaxation and to a feeling of inner comfort and pleasure. If one learns and practices the extended series of progressive relaxation exercises, he can relax the body to such a degree that he experiences sheer delight. Sensory pleasure is an adumbrated form, an imperfect expression, of that delight. It points the way to a more complete and fulfilling ecstasy. One can learn to luxuriate in a degree of pleasure that is greater and more comforting than that which is found through temporarily merging with an external object of desire. The delight experienced through yogic progressive relaxation is like basking in the warmth and comfort of an inner sun. One feels that he is living in the lap of luxury. That subtle yet intense pleasure experienced within is itself only an imperfect approximation, a prefiguring, of the ecstasy that can be experienced as one carries relaxation beyond his musculature to ever more subtle aspects of his being, including relaxation of the mind.

Mystics throughout the ages have described such ecstatic states but have usually offered little in the way of systematic means for attaining those states. In most instances, the mystics had little ability to control their experiences. They were overwhelmed by states of ecstasy that came upon them for no reason that they could discern. However, yoga science systematically teaches one how to regulate his states of consciousness. Yoga relaxation can progressively lead to the state of *yoga nidra,* in which the body is in an extremely relaxed state comparable to that of deep sleep while the person remains conscious in a state of bliss.[13] Though that experience is attained only by a fortunate few who have mastered the yogic techniques of progressive relaxation, even those who master the beginning techniques of muscular relaxation will come upon an inner state of inherent pleasure, the existence of which they had not previously known.

In order to know those states, one must learn to turn inward, to experience the joy radiating within. That joy is ever so subtle compared with the coarse, dense, noisy experiences that come from contact with the external world. As one relaxes, quiets himself, and learns to tune in to his inner state, that dim, far-off radiance will shine with ever greater intensity, until one finds himself at the center of radiant bliss. He will attain a state of ecstasy many times more intense than the pleasure that can be experienced through sensory channels.

One cannot turn inward toward that internal ecstasy unless he lets go of his preoccupying desire for external objects. Thus the yogic teachings encourage one to give up desire and thereby experience joy:

> When a man dwells on the pleasures of sense, attraction for them arises in him. From attraction arises desire, the lust of possession, and this leads to passion, to anger.

> From passion comes confusion of mind, then loss of remembrance, the forgetting of duty. From this loss comes the ruin of reason, and the ruin of reason leads man to destruction.

> But the soul that moves in the world of the senses and yet keeps the senses in harmony, free from attraction and aversion, finds rest in quietness.

> In this quietness falls down the burden of all her sorrows, for when the heart has found quietness, wisdom has also found peace. There is no wisdom for a man without harmony, and without harmony there is no contemplation. Without contemplation there cannot be peace, and without peace can there be joy?[14]

Tantra philosophy and psychology emphasize the second chakra as a motivating force. In the tantric system, one's latent energy (kundalini) is depicted as a coiled serpent that has its home at the second chakra. Tantra recognizes the importance of respecting this archetype rather than suppressing its expression. In tantric practices, one's latent energy is awakened, made available to consciousness, transmuted, and expressed through more evolved centers. In less evolved tantric schools, one may engage with the objects that ordinarily lead to the experience of sensory pleasure. While maintaining contact with the objects, he learns to stop identifying with the sensate pleasure and to thereby experience more subtle forms of ecstasy. Through this process one becomes a master of the sensory realm rather than its captive.

Yoga is not puritanical; it does not lead one to deny the second chakra mode of experience. Rather it seeks to refine that mode of experience, leading one to more profound and complete experiences of joy and ecstasy. The sensory channels are limited in the degree and type of pleasure that they can transmit, but the capacity of one's consciousness to experience bliss knows no limit.

## MASTERY

At the first and second chakras, one ordinarily identifies solely with his physical body. Since the body is fragile and subject to injury, disease, and death, suffering is inevitable when one is enmeshed in those modes of experience. At the third chakra, manipura, one extends his territory to include what he owns and that for which he is responsible. The scenarios at this chakra are created from one's absorption in defining, maintaining, and expanding his territory and achieving control over his dominion. Here one replaces the pursuit of pleasure with concerns about mastery and power. He views others as adversaries or rivals and becomes absorbed in such issues as success and failure, dominance and submission, heroism and cowardice, conquering and being conquered. This third mode of consciousness is the realm of the ego. One seeks to prove himself by outdoing others and by gaining power, prestige, and recognition. He is absorbed in politics both in his personal life and in his relationship with the world at large. Manipulation, coercion, and conniving are characteristic behaviors in the scenarios created out of this archetype. A person operating on this level is goal-oriented; he has difficulty being in the present moment. From his perspective, even spiritual experiences are attainments to be achieved and gloated over by the ego.

Psychological theories, rather than being objective descriptions of the functioning of the psyche, are created by human beings and reflect the biases and limited perspectives of their creators. Every theory reflects its founder's personality, conflicts, scenarios, and preoccupations. Thus if the founder of a theory is himself thoroughly enmeshed in one particular archetypal realm, his theory will describe the psyche in terms of that mode of functioning: "We can... discern a dominant archetype underlying the doctrines of the various ... psychologists. When Freud sees the beginning and principle of everything that happens in sexuality, Adler in the striving for power, these two are ideas expressing ... archetypal representations."[15]

Thus it is not surprising that psychological theorists who look at the world from the perspective of the second chakra do not consider the development of the ego to be a positive step in one's evolution. Indeed, one of the founders of bioenergetic therapy, Alexander Lowen, so highly values the experience of sensory pleasure that he has written: "The domination of the personality by the ego is a diabolical perversion of the nature of man. The ego was never intended to be the master of the body, but its loyal and obedient servant. The body, as opposed to the ego, desires pleasure, not power. Bodily pleasure is the source from which all our good feelings and good thinking stems."[16]

By contrast, theorists such as Alfred Adler, Robert W.

White, and other ego psychologists consider ego development to be the measure of man. Those theorists take the perspective of ego-consciousness, and they lucidly describe the psychology of one who is absorbed in the ego archetype. They are able to understand the dilemmas, anxieties, and preoccupations of such a person, but they may have considerable difficulty in understanding someone who is functioning from another archetype. Their therapies help one to build his ego, to replace submissiveness with assertiveness, failure with success, and a sense of inferiority with the experience of being capable and competent. Such changes occur within the framework of ego-consciousness. They lead to the substitution of one role with its reciprocal within the same drama. The plot remains focused on failure and success, competence and incompetence, top dog and underdog, master and slave.

Those who are functioning in this mode and who play the role of being powerful, successful, dominant, or heroic are not likely to find their way into the therapist's consulting room. If the egoist experiences internal conflict, he is likely to avoid psychotherapy. He likes to tackle problems on his own, and looks upon those who go to a therapist as weak. Because of his felt need to assert control and authority, when and if he does find himself in psychotherapy or marital counseling, it will likely be for only a short time.

It is the person at the other end of this polarity—he who is timid and insecure, who feels inadequate in jousting with the world—who tends to seek the support, encouragement, or guidance of a counselor or psychotherapist. Such a person is caught up in a vicious cycle. He feels inadequate, so he becomes preoccupied with gaining approval from others. He is afraid that if others find out how inadequate he is, they will reject him. So he hides. He neither expresses his inner feelings nor acts. He remains frozen. As a result, he fails to get the acclaim he seeks and is often snubbed by others, who find him to be lacking in vitality and spontaneity. His feelings of inadequacy are thus confirmed, leading to further self-doubt, hesitation, and ineptness. Here are two examples of this mode of being:

C1: *I have this inhibition. I'm not able to go on a date and feel comfortable. I always want to make sure that my date has a good time. I want to keep an image. I'm also afraid that she might gossip; she might say that I'm boring or dull. I want others to have positive reactions toward me. I'm always trying to please.*

C2: *I want to be able to take risks, like getting up in front of a group and feeling that it's okay to mess up. But if I were to screw up, there would be a lot of people who would laugh or gossip. I even feel that way when I'm with a group of friends and it's time for me to leave. I feel that I'm on the spot and I have to really produce. I have to get up and say good-bye to them. I want to make it look a certain way. I want to have control and I want to impress the person I'm saying good-bye to. But I'm afraid that I might screw it up.*

*I was going to call a girl on the phone last night. All of a sudden, there she'd be on the phone and I'd have to talk to her, so I was hesitating. The week before, I saw her at a bar and I wanted to meet her. I was in a little panic. Then after my friend introduced us, I tried to talk, but my mind was thinking, Don't blow it. Don't say the wrong thing. Don't lose control. Don't panic. I was afraid that I would mess up. It's pretty hard to carry on a conversation with all those thoughts going through your mind. My heart was pounding, and I wanted to run away.*

Some people feel a greater sense of adequacy, but have not yet learned to assert themselves. The following client, who is attempting to overcome her timidity, is such a person:

At times at work, someone will criticize what I'm doing—my boss will make some kind of negative comment about something that I've done. Sometimes he'll be accusative, which I suppose has certain benefits for him: he keeps in control and power. I'm usually timid about responding.

> I'm always surprised in situations where people take advantage of me. I'm generally taken aback without knowing how to respond. But I'm learning to be more assertive. This week I had a talk with my neighbor. She's been playing her stereo very loud for months. I finally told her it disturbed me. She said, "Okay, I'll keep it turned down." I feel a need to be more assertive. I have always let my husband deal with neighbors up until now. This is the first time that I have said anything. I walked right up to her door and I talked to her. And she said, "I don't blame you. I would be angry, too." I feel more responsible and have more respect for myself.

In this mode of consciousness, one is concerned with establishing, maintaining, and expanding what he regards as his territory. Two common character types that epitomize this way of being are the entrepreneur and the bureaucrat. The bureaucrat primarily seeks to maintain his territory, while the entrepreneur seeks to take over more territory. When a person operating from this level of consciousness believes that his territory is being threatened or invaded, he typically reacts with anger. Here is an example:

> When I was in the hospital, I asked to have no visitors. Everyone respected that, except the woman I work with. She walked right into the hospital room. I was furious. It was an invasion of my privacy and disrespectful. I had made it very clear to everyone: "no visitors." The door was closed, which I thought gave me some control over who would walk in. But she walked in anyway, so I felt that I had lost control. She does the same thing at work: I'm in a room with the door closed and she just bursts in. I become enraged.

Many people fail to distinguish between aggression and assertiveness. Their characteristic response to being invaded or verbally attacked is to retaliate, to answer tit for tat by calling names or in some way attacking the other person. Some people, however, afraid of their own aggressiveness, hold back their anger for fear of losing control. In yoga therapy, one learns to distinguish between assertiveness (moving the other person out of one's territory) and aggressiveness (invading another's territory).

Children are often taught that expressing anger is unacceptable, so they learn not to express it. As adults they may habitually keep their anger to themselves, and also discount and devalue their emotions and other feelings. Such people value what others think and feel above their own experience. Wanting to be accepted even by a person who is being invasive, they do not express their anger or defend their territory. Many of these people have so successfully cut themselves off from their anger that they are not even aware of their own physiological and emotional responses to the invasion of their territory.

Many approaches to psychotherapy help clients to get in touch with their anger. The client may be encouraged to experience the depth of his rage and to express it both physically and verbally in therapy. While it is important to recover emotions that have been repressed, this is only an intermediate step in the expansion of consciousness. Identifying with one's anger can also leave one mired in a particular plot line and closed to other ways of being. Yoga therapy does not encourage one to be passive or to deny his emotions; it helps one to recover repressed anger, but it also goes further to help one gain a perspective on the anger rather than identifying with it. The following client, who suffered from an asthmatic condition, is struggling with this issue:

C: My mother-in-law came to visit and she started to change my plans around. I had promised to help someone, but she wanted to go shopping. I did rearrange things, but the whole day was negative; everything that came up I was against. I couldn't seemingly do anything about it. Evidently, I was very resentful and angry that I had to change my plans.

T: *You say you* had *to?*

C: *I didn't feel that there was anything I could do. It would have been much easier for me if I had been able to express my anger. I didn't do that. I didn't know how to do it without somehow becoming involved in the anger. I still am not able to look at a situation that makes me angry rather than being right in it. I can't get above it and see it objectively. I was angry that she was invading my space. I don't think that she realized that she was imposing on me.*

T: *Did you tell her that you felt invaded?*

C: *No, I really didn't know how to go about approaching her and saying, "You are invading my space." Not get angry, but just say it without causing more problems because of my emotions.*

T: *I just thought of an interesting phrase: "getting it off your chest." It seems to me that if you would assert yourself when you first sense someone invading or taking over, you wouldn't be nearly as emotional. But if you let it go on, it seems that your emotions intensify. This situation showed you that you can't escape from your anger. If you don't express yourself, it's going to come out another way— through negativity or through physical symptoms. In a sense, you got it off your chest by being negative.*

C: *Yes, but I really didn't, because that wasn't satisfying. The only thing that would have helped was to withdraw myself completely.*

T: *I wonder if that would really help. I think it would be better to say directly what it is that is bothering you as soon as you become aware of it. Then you wouldn't be holding on to the anger and turning it into resentment and tension for yourself. Then perhaps you could resolve the issue and move on.*

From the perspective of the more evolved archetypes, the territorial boundaries drawn in the first three chakras do not really exist. However, the majority of people in modern society experience the world primarily through the first three chakras, so it is important for them to deal with territorial distinctions effectively. Instead of being mutually invasive and waging internecine war, two individuals can learn to respect each other's personal autonomy. Eventually they may recognize themselves as part of a more comprehensive system in which they share common goals, rather than experiencing themselves as adversaries or combatants. This sort of shift in perspective occurs when one moves from the third to the fourth mode of consciousness.

The development of ego capacities, including the ability to assert oneself, is a necessary step in the evolution of consciousness; it is important that a person be able to function competently in the world. However, difficulties arise when one identifies with his accomplishments, just as they do when he thinks of himself as inadequate and incompetent. One can remain stuck in this mode of consciousness at either end of a polarity.

Lowen pointed out that egoistic consciousness may stifle one's capacity to experience pleasure. He encourages a way out of identification with the ego by regressing to the pleasure principle and asserting its sovereignty over the ego. Yoga therapy offers another path, not well trodden in modern psychology: it encourages one to move forward to a more evolved mode of consciousness, in which preoccupations with such questions as success and failure, top dog and underdog, are left behind, while the capacities of the ego for mastery are still retained. Lowen is correct insofar as he asserts that the capacity for pleasure is not to be abandoned with the development of ego-consciousness; and in a similar way ego capacities are not to be abandoned as one becomes absorbed in the next archetype. Instead, as one reaches a more evolved mode of experiencing, he becomes able to play the various roles generated in the less evolved modes with increased mastery and greater flexibility.

The yoga therapist encourages and assists those who need to develop and strengthen their egos to do so; however, if a client becomes identified with this archetype to the exclusion of higher modes of awareness, the therapist will lead the client toward the experience of those other realms. For while this third archetypal mode of experience represents a step forward in the development of consciousness toward greater rationality, mastery, and responsibility, it is only an intermediate attainment.

Modern society encourages one to become identified with the first three modes of consciousness. The focus on first-chakra concerns in the news and in movies has already been mentioned. The emphasis that society places on the second-chakra desire for attaining sensory gratification through sex, eating, intoxicants, and other means of stimulating the senses is obvious, as is its accentuation of the third-chakra focus on acquisitiveness, control, competition, gambling, self-aggrandizement, and so on. These three modes of being lead one to experience considerable discomfort, anxiety, and distress, along with the more positive experiences of security, sensory pleasure, and mastery. In comparison with the more evolved modes of being, the degree of joy, harmony, and fulfillment experienced in these realms is quite limited. Yet these lower modes are integral aspects of the overall design of being and do have their value in leading one up the ladder of evolution to greater consciousness of oneself and to ever more self-responsibility. Even at further stages of development, they may continue to remain meaningful realms of experience in the service of more evolved modes of being.

## PSYCHOSOMATIC DISORDERS

The system of chakras helps one to understand how particular mental-emotional states are directly related to and experienced in specific parts of the body. A disturbance in a bodily function can be understood as a physical manifestation of a disturbance in the psychological functioning related to a specific chakra; that is, an archetypal theme being enacted at a particular chakra can lead to a disturbance in the part of the body that corresponds to that chakra. Many psychosomatic and physical disorders can be better understood and treated more successfully if the therapist is aware of the archetypal theme that is being played out through a somatic dysfunction. For example, colitis, diarrhea, and other bowel problems can occur as a result of the fear and anxiety experienced in the first-chakra mode of consciousness.

Likewise, any of a number of various stomach disorders can result from one's involvement in the egoistic mode of consciousness. One who is preoccupied with self-worth, who experiences jealousy and envy of those who have what he does not, or who has difficulty in establishing or maintaining his territory, is likely to experience ulcers and other stomach problems. Many stomach disorders are a result of liver dysfunction, and in this regard the Greek myth of Prometheus is highly instructive. In Greek mythology, Prometheus symbolizes the egoistic consciousness of the manipura chakra. Prometheus stole fire for mankind from the realm of the gods. Instead of assuming a devotional attitude and acknowledging the superiority of the heavenly realm, Prometheus attempted to make man an equal of the gods. As retribution for this hubris, he was chained to a rock, where a vulture ate at his liver. This myth is, among other things, a symbolic explanation of the psychical origin of liver dysfunction. It informs us that one who lives by his ego and fails to acknowledge that which transcends the ego robs himself of nourishment from the heavenly realm. This is expressed even at the physical level, where the malfunctioning liver at the navel center does not allow the nutrients ingested at the throat center, the center of nurturance, to be assimilated. A person who identifies with his ego, who seeks to control others, who is demanding and easily angered if his demands are not met, may well experience a liver disorder. Indeed, the word "jaundiced" refers both to one who is embittered, hostile, and envious, and to one who has a liver dysfunction.

The person whose liver is not functioning properly may consume a great deal of nutritious food and yet feel undernourished. He may even come to believe that he has a tapeworm that consumes the nutrients he needs. And in a sense he does: his ego is the tapeworm. The ego is a parasite that derives its sustenance from the Self. Although it draws its nourishment from the Self, the ego has no regard for its host. It attempts to assert its sovereignty, and in so doing deprives the person of the nourishment that flows from the Self. In many cases, liver dysfunction can be ameliorated by rising to a more evolved mode of consciousness. At the heart center, one is transformed from a parasite to a servant, and the liver no longer plays a central role in his life drama. If one rises to the level of vishuddha consciousness at the throat center, he experiences the nourishment that was lacking in manipura consciousness.

Asthma is another condition that results from a disturbance at manipura. Whereas the person with a bilious or choleric temperament aggressively asserts his ego, the asthmatic is likely to be at the other extreme, not asserting himself sufficiently. The asthmatic typically takes no corrective action when he feels pressed or suffocated by another: he neither flees, nor does he fight to defend the autonomy of his territory. He does not allow himself to fully experience the resentment or anger he feels; he doesn't "get things off his chest." This way of being is reflected in a disturbance of physical functioning at manipura. For an asthmatic, the adrenal glands, which are located in the region of the manipura chakra, do not secrete enough adrenalin. This hormone helps to energize an animal or a human being, and its secretion is integral to the fight-or-flight reaction. The asthmatic lacks the charge of energy that the adrenal glands provide. In some cases cortisone, another hormone from the adrenal glands, is used to treat asthma.

Other conditions related to disturbances in the third chakra include anorexia nervosa and bulimia, which are also related to issues in the fifth chakra. The personality of the anorexic clearly reflects a third-chakra mode of being: anorexics are frequently described as controlled, perfectionistic, stubborn, and conscientious. Their symptomatic behavior often begins when they feel inadequate because life changes are requiring new skills with which they are unfamiliar. Anorexics deny themselves the experience of being nurtured.

Bulimics exhibit a conflict between feeling helpless and a need to be independent, between the wish to surrender to a source of nurturance and a distrust of that source. They are hungry for nurturance, but they find that no matter how much they gorge themselves, they are never satisfied. A bulimic craves parental love and acceptance but is likely to have experienced repeated rejection and thus feels unlovable. Though the parents of a bulimic may verbally express their love for their child, the child is convinced that they actually have little or no love for him. As adults, bulimics continue to feel that they are despicable, and their behavior reflects and perpetuates this self-concept. For such people food symbolizes the love and acceptance they long for, but they can no more stomach the food they ingest than they can stomach their parents' protestations of love, which they experience as insincere. The bulimic both craves food and rejects it as though it were poison. He vomits up the poisoned nurturance and then again compulsively gorges himself with more, only to vomit it up once again.

In helping a client to correct these and other physical and behavioral disorders, the yoga therapist leads the client to become aware of the underlying psychological disturbance and its symbolic aspects and to modify the scenario that is perpetuating the disturbance. He may ask the client to do mental exercises in which the client concentrates on the chakra that is related to the disturbed functioning. Concentration on a particular center helps to energize that center and bring the disturbance to the foreground of one's consciousness, where it can be more readily resolved.

## SERVICE

The first three modes of consciousness lead to the various unpleasant emotional states experienced by human beings, such as fear, anxiety, frustration, anger, jealousy, envy, greed, and depression. At the fourth chakra, anahata, those emotions are left behind, and the egocentric perspective of the third chakra is also transcended. At the fourth chakra, one comes out of the underworld and into the light. He undergoes a revolution of perspective: leaving the realm in which struggle, secrecy, conniving, and self-aggrandizement prevail, he comes into the warm, radiant sunshine of caring for others. He now lives by the principle that is the complement of that found in the first three chakras. No longer either fearing that something will be taken away or striving to attain and hold on to what one thinks he needs, he experiences a sense of fullness within himself and seeks to share his abundance with others. Grabbing and clutching are replaced by generosity. At the more primitive chakras, one feels in need and is concerned for himself alone, but at anahata, one does not care for his needs. Instead, he feels the needs of others and becomes salve to their hurts. He is truly a friend or parent to all.

The fourth chakra, at the heart center, is midway in the journey toward unitary consciousness. At the three more primitive chakras that lie below this center, one involves himself in and identifies with the material forms. As one evolves through the chakras, he first learns to cease identifying with the most gross or material existence, and then to progressively let go of his identification with ever more subtle forms and to draw nearer to the experience of unitary consciousness. At the heart center, one moves from preoccupations with his body, senses, and territory to a new focus on that which transcends the individual.

When a person whose consciousness is at muladhara encounters someone else, his thoughts revolve around survival issues; when a person functioning from svadhisthana meets another, he is interested in whether he can receive pleasure from the other; when a person operating from manipura interacts with another, he is concerned about who will have power and control. Such people are concerned solely with their own needs and desires; they are interested in and concerned for others only insofar as others can help them obtain their own wants. But a person functioning from the heart center has a different way of relating to others. When he encounters another person, he asks himself how he may serve that person. Instead of being absorbed in his own needs, he is interested in meeting the needs of others. At the heart center, one becomes transformed from a person who takes to a person who is generous. In giving, he finds a greater joy than he experienced in taking, for a person who takes carries the attitude that he is incomplete and in need, while in giving one comes in touch with that which he has.

The word "love" is often used in describing one's experience at this chakra. But this word has been misused so often and debased so much that it is not adequate to convey the emotion experienced at the heart center. As one moves from one chakra to another, each symbol or concept is reinterpreted and given an entirely new meaning. When one is functioning at a lower chakra, he interprets the words used to describe higher-chakra experiences in terms of the perspective of his level of functioning. For example, a person functioning at muladhara explained that he followed the golden rule, which he interpreted as, "Do it to them before they do it to you." Similarly, those who are functioning at a lower center misunderstand love in terms of the consciousness of that center. For example, the word "love" is often used to express the sensory desires of the second chakra. We say, "I love ice cream" or "I love the way silk feels." The word "love" is also used to express the acquisitiveness characteristic of the third chakra. Here one "loves" his possessions. In these modes of consciousness, one has expectations of that which he "loves." One "loves" another person or an object because it fulfills his needs. If the person or object does not meet his expectations, such "love" can easily turn to hatred or indifference.

One may do something for another, claiming that he is doing it because he loves that person, but actually doing it because he expects the person to do something for him in return. If his expectation is not met, he complains, "Look what I did for you, and you couldn't even do this one thing for me." Such doing with expectations is not love as it is experienced through the heart center. Such actions are based on an implied contract: "If I do something for you, you will do something for me." An agreement of this sort has its place, but it is unfortunate if one takes such an exchange to be love, for then he is missing the genuine experience.

The word "love" as it is used by those functioning at the lower chakras focuses on what the object of love is doing or can do for the person who "loves" that object. But in love as it is experienced at the anahata chakra, there is no thought of receiving. Such love is giving, giving, giving. One dissolves his sense of separateness in giving, so there is no thought of return. When functioning from the lower chakras, one feels incomplete and seeks something to make him feel complete, but at the anahata chakra, one's fullness overflows to nourish others.

The sun is a symbol of the heart chakra, for the sun nurtures all living things on earth. It radiates continuously in all directions and does not discriminate in any way; all living things receive its life-giving light. And what does the sun seek in return for the energy and warmth it gives? So far no one has ever received an energy bill from the sun. Neither has the sun sent a message threatening that it will not shine unless everyone bows down, worships it, and lives according to its dictates. The sun radiates energy and light and nourishes us because that is its nature—that is the way the sun expresses itself.

Most people place limits on the extent to which they give. They are concerned that if they give too much, they will become depleted. And if they do give, they are interested in what they will receive in return. Such "giving" is not an experience of the fourth chakra, but rather a bargain made in the insecurity of a lower mode of experience. One is concerned that he will be taken advantage of if he gives too much or does not get something in return. If he does not receive something of a material nature, he will seek recognition or appreciation from others or will praise himself for being a kind person.

In the way of the heart center, however, one has no such concerns. He is interested in providing what is needed and does not want appreciation or recognition. He may even prefer to give anonymously. At the heart center, the lower-chakra feeling that one is lacking what he needs is replaced with the experience of abundance. The more one freely gives, the more abundance he experiences, and in turn, the more he is able to give.

This way of being makes no sense to the person living within the perspective of the third chakra. He is convinced that the person who gives so abundantly will eventually become depleted or break down. He does not consider this to be a viable way of living in the modern world. He thinks that those who function from the heart center will be hurt and abused; he believes that one must of necessity be "tough" in dealing with the harsh world he perceives.

In the first three chakras, the two sides of a polarity are experienced as being distinct from or in opposition to one another, but at the heart center, one begins to understand the complementary relationship between the two sides of a polarity. Instead of projecting his opposite, as in the first three chakras, at anahata one becomes aware that the distinction between himself and others is artificial and unreal. He realizes that in giving to others, he is giving to himself, that in treating others, he is treating himself. He experiences warmth and joy in giving, but only uneasiness and discomfort in grasping and holding on.

Those who have not reached this center are unaware of the paradoxical twist in the nature of giving and taking. Genuine giving never depletes itself, whereas no matter how much one takes, he will never feel satisfied. Giving never empties itself; taking never leads to feeling full. The only way to experience fullness is to give everything.

When a person remains in the lower chakras, he continually seeks to maintain or enhance himself. He may want to take in pleasurable experiences, to possess more and more, or to have increased power over others. But he actually depletes his energy on all levels through worries, preoccupations, nervousness, and emotional turmoil. He remains in a state of confusion and agitation, caught in a vicious cycle. For the more one is oriented toward self-advancement and self-aggrandizement, the more he notices what he needs and does not have, the more upset and emotional he becomes, and the more he feels the need to take in order to be satisfied. But at the heart center, this vicious cycle is replaced with a cycle that leads to abundance: the more one gives, the more joy, fulfillment, and completeness he experiences, and the more he has to give.

One need not give up egoistic functioning as he ascends to the heart center. He can continue to use that mode of consciousness as a tool in the service of the more evolved mode of being. For example, one who genuinely wishes to serve may find it helpful to have a building to care for others, to train assistants who work under his guidance, and to have an organization in order to carry out his work more effectively. One may adopt a provisional egoistic perspective in order to function competently in serving others.

When individuals functioning through the less evolved archetypes predominate in a society, that society is characterized by such qualities as brutality, promiscuity, coercion, competition, politicking, and outsized bureaucratic structure for maintaining security. Such societies, no matter how much they may esteem themselves for their apparent accomplishments, have not yet developed a genuine concern for human beings. Humanism dawns when consciousness reaches and is expressed through the heart center. A society composed of individuals functioning at this center will be interested in the welfare and self-actualization of all its members.

At the heart center, the humanistic paradigm comes to the fore. One values human well-being and is concerned with nurturing human potentials. Carl Rogers, with his emphasis on empathic understanding and unconditional positive regard, has developed an approach to psychotherapy founded on this mode of experience. Rogers's person-centered approach helps to free therapists from a more authoritarian third-chakra orientation. Likewise, Erich Fromm's teachings focus on the transition from a preoccupation with mastery and power to the expression of love. Fromm encourages the development of such qualities as a willingness to give up all forms of having, in order to fully *be*; a joy that comes from giving and sharing, not from hoarding and exploiting; an ever-developing capacity for love; and a shedding of narcissism.[17]

In many cases, a client's conflict and dissatisfaction result from dwelling on himself and what he perceives as his unfulfilled needs. Such a person believes that he will be happier when he finds a way to satisfy those needs, but such satisfaction is never attained. As long as one is oriented in this way, he will always find needs that are not met, and he will continue to feel unfulfilled. The only way out of this predicament is to cease to be concerned about one's needs and to become interested in the needs of others. The following two clients who have been in yoga therapy describe such a shift from an acquisitive third-chakra orientation to a loving, nurturing way of being:

C1: *I want to quit dwelling on myself. There has been a feeling in me of wanting to hold and retain what I have, a fear of letting go. I've been very fearful of giving what I have. But I experience a cer-*

*tain sense of freedom and gladness when I help people. When I have experienced giving, I've liked it. There seems to be a change in my attitude from deficiency, feeling I might be depleted, to the feeling that I have plenty left over for me and others, too.*

*C2: I want to use my knowledge in a way that is not egotistical but is worthwhile to other people. As soon as I start doing that, I'll feel that I'm a useful member of this universe instead of constantly being on my own trip and feeling like a self-centered unity, locked up in this box I call "me." Until I do that, I'm not going to be satisfied. I've been very self-centered; I've done very little in terms of really being out in the world and giving. And until now, when I did give, I'd expect something in return—to know that someone would think well of me. But I don't want to give in that way. Giving should be sufficient in itself. I want to move away from my self-centeredness. I want to develop more of a sense of selflessness and doing service.*

*Until now, I've been insecure. I've felt that unless I attained certain things, I would have nothing to give. I would think, Unless I'm this and this and this, how can I possibly give? What do I have to give? But I'm beginning to realize that there is always something to give; you can never run out of things to give. There are a lot of things a person could do even without some special qualifications, like being a big brother or just doing something for your neighbor or your wife just for the sake of giving. I want to do more of that type of thing. The more I love, the more I'll be in touch with love, and the more I'll have to give.*

Family life teaches one this giving and caring mode of being. It requires the sacrifice of one's own desires, service to others, and the development of empathy. When one finds himself with children to care for, he learns to be generous and self-sacrificing. Many people are transformed from an absorption in the third-chakra mode of consciousness to a fourth-chakra perspective through their relationships with their children.

When one begins to function from the heart center, his way of relating with others undergoes a dramatic reversal. Thus, whereas two people functioning from the perspective of the third chakra might fight each other because they both desire the same object, two people operating from the fourth chakra would each be concerned with the other's welfare, and not their own. In this regard the story is told of a young man and an elderly man who, during a famine, were arguing on the street over a loaf of bread. A third man approached them to intervene. He said, "Shame on you, fighting over food. Can't you share it?" The young man replied, "I don't want to share it. I'm strong and can go for days without food. This man is old and very weak from hunger. If he doesn't eat, he may die. I insist he take this loaf of bread." Whereupon the older man retorted, "He is young and has many years before him. It is better that he eat and live. I will die soon anyway. Please convince him to take this loaf."

This story conveys the attitude of the heart chakra. There are many shining examples of those who have sacrificed self-interest—in some cases, even their lives—in order to nurture others. Living a life of service to others, they have experienced a peace and joy that is found only in this mode of consciousness. Mother Teresa of Calcutta is a contemporary exemplar of one who has experienced the fullness of giving.

The songwriter Bob Dylan noted that even those who are most identified with mastery, power, and ownership are involved in service in some aspect of their lives. One of his songs states:

> You might own guns.
> And you might even own tanks:
> You might be somebody's landlord,
> You might even own banks—
> But you're gonna have to serve somebody,
> Yes, you're gonna have to serve somebody.[18]

During the course of a day, most people perform many services for others. For example the mailman, bus driver, garbage collector, politician, accountant, assembly-line worker, all serve many people each working day. But many of these workers remain oblivious to the service they are performing. They are working for a reward: their paycheck and the objects and experiences it will buy. If their job is routine, they may feel little sense of accomplishment or self-worth. Thus they perform their work with inattention and carelessness while dwelling on fantasies of pleasure or attainment. If, however, they were to focus on the service they are performing, even the most menial job would be experienced as meaningful and of great worth.

The view that some work is more significant and of greater worth than other work is an attitude of the third chakra, where weighing and comparing are important. At the fourth chakra, one has no interest in such comparisons, for his energy and enthusiasm are directed toward being of greater service. The bus driver or mailman operating from the perspective of the anahata chakra will take care to serve his patrons as best he can. He will be concerned for their interests rather than his reward. Working with this attitude, he may be surprised to find himself doubly rewarded where he sought no reward at all: he will be rewarded by the joy he experiences in serving and also by the unsought material rewards that are likely to accrue when one does his job well and with care.

There are various yogic practices that cultivate the modes of being found in the fourth through the seventh chakras. Karma yoga, the yoga of action, leads one to experience the fourth archetypal mode of consciousness. In karma yoga, one is taught to do actions as a service.[19] The *Bhagavad Gita* teaches:

> Do thy work in the peace of Yoga and, free from selfish desires, be not moved in success or in failure .... Even as the unwise work selfishly in the bondage of selfish works, let the wise man work unselfishly for the good of all the world.[20]

This way of being is not imposed on the student of yoga, for inculcation of selfless precepts is ineffective and even harmful if one is not ready to make the transition to this mode of consciousness. Far too many children have been taught by parents, educators, and religious teachers with the best of intentions that self-interest and assertiveness is bad and that they should be selfless, giving, and loving. Rather than being encouraged to grow through the stage of ego development, they have had a more mature perspective forced upon them before they have been ready to assimilate it. As a result, it becomes necessary for them as adults to retrace their steps and acknowledge and accept those egoistic qualities in themselves that they had long denied. One must learn to establish boundaries and a territory and to assert himself before he can move to later stages in the evolution of consciousness. He must first define himself and take responsibility for himself before he can give himself in serving another. If he does not, he will merely develop an outward persona, a false front, of being loving and generous; he will mimic this way of being while inwardly remaining in that earlier mode of consciousness that he was not allowed to experience fully. Yoga therapy assists at each stage in this evolutionary journey. It helps one to recover emotions, to develop assertiveness and ego capacities, and then to progress beyond identification with the egoistic mode of being.

Although identifying with the fourth-chakra mode of consciousness leads to a more radiant and loving life, it is still far from the most evolved state of consciousness. One operating from the heart center still may experience incompleteness and discontent. Though one is reaching beyond himself, he still experiences the world from a dualistic frame of reference. The scenarios that are played out at the anahata chakra require a helper and a person who needs aid, comfort, and nurturance. For one to experience and enact those dramas, discomfort and suffering must exist in the world, so that one can provide aid and comfort and partially alleviate suffering.

In still more evolved states of consciousness, those limitations are also transcended.

One may believe that the love he shares emanates from him, that it is his love. But when this mode of being is used in the service of the more evolved chakras, one comes to understand that he is merely an instrument for the love that is flowing through him from a more comprehensive center of being. By emptying himself of his egoistic concerns, he makes himself a clear channel through which the love of the Supreme may flow unimpeded.

# Chapter Five

# SPIRITUAL ASPECTS OF PSYCHOTHERAPY

AT THE FOURTH CHAKRA, THE HEART CENTER, one begins the transition from egoistic consciousness to a new mode of being that recognizes and is guided by a far more inclusive center of organization than the ego. In the first three modes of consciousness, he learns to define himself as a distinct being and to function in terms of his limited self-definition. As the ego develops at the third chakra, it helps to lift one out of the elemental fear and impulsiveness that can plague one in the first two modes of consciousness; the unfoldment of the ego enables one to cope in the world. However, the ego itself can become an obstruction to further progress. It stands as a barrier at the threshold of the evolutionary phase of development. When the ego attempts to assert its supremacy, it restricts one from consciously reorganizing around a more comprehensive center.

Modern psychotherapy is primarily oriented around the development and strengthening of the ego, and this is quite appropriate for those who are struggling to free themselves from the preoccupations of the more primitive levels of consciousness. As we have seen, yoga therapy also helps people functioning at those levels to develop ego capacities. However, current models of psychotherapy generally neglect to help one reach beyond identification with the ego, whereas yoga therapy is especially beneficial in this latter phase of development.

A person typically identifies with the ego and the extremely limited attributes that the ego has taken upon itself; he considers himself to be, for example, good-looking, shy, lazy, competent, absentminded, and so on. Psychotherapy helps one modify his definition of himself; attributes that are considered to be more positive or that fit more closely with the demands of the social or natural environment are gradually substituted for those that have caused acute distress. As a result of psychotherapy, a person may begin to define himself as capable and lovable or in terms of other attributes that are considered to be positive. But even an ego that identifies with positive attributes remains fundamentally insecure and seeks to bolster itself by manipulating the external environment. One acquires possessions and power, yet he continues to suffer as a result of demands, expectations, frustrations, disappointments, and various emotional states. Changes in the attributes associated with the ego may temporarily diminish one's sense of unhappiness to a limited degree, but such surface modifications have no effect on the underlying cause of unhappiness. Human suffering cannot be eliminated by this process.

According to the dualistic and monistic paradigms, all human suffering is ultimately the result of spiritual impoverishment, that is, non-awareness of transcendent being. Psychotherapies that do not foster this awareness are at best a means for temporarily holding suffering at bay. Therapies that help to strengthen the ego are fine in their place, but therapies are also needed that lead a person beyond identification with the ego and that help him become aware of a more integrative center of consciousness. The therapist who is unable to help the client recognize this dimension of life is severely restricted in his ability to help his client grow.

Many aspects of life that are difficult for clients to face are dealt with in the accepting atmosphere of the therapist's consulting room. For instance, many clients learn to come to terms with their sexuality or aggression. Yet strangely enough, the open exploration of spiritual concerns still remains taboo for the majority of psychotherapists. A number of clients who had previously been in psychotherapy have told me that when they tried to deal with spiritual concerns, the therapist was unable to work with them in a way that respected and affirmed the spiritual aspect of life. There are a significant number of people who feel a need for psychotherapy but who do not seek out a therapist because they believe that the typical therapist has little regard for spirituality. Many of these people also avoid pastoral counseling because they do not want to be directed toward a particular religious dogma. They find themselves in the dark limbo between reductionist psychology and religious institutionalism, limited to a choice between psychotherapy that ignores the spiritual dimension of life and counseling that incorporates religious dogma. It is important that psychotherapeutic approaches be developed that encourage one to explore and discover for himself his relation to transcendent being.

There is a legitimate concern among psychotherapists that a clear distinction be maintained between psychotherapy and religion. It is, however, unfortunate that most psychotherapists have not yet learned that it is possible to deal with spiritual issues outside the context of religious institutionalism. It is possible to develop a spiritually based psychotherapy that respects the client's own developing awareness of transcendent being without imposing belief in a particular form of God, means of worship, or religious dogma.

In yoga therapy, a consideration of the spiritual dimension of life is the foundation of the therapeutic process; it is the substratum upon which all the therapeutic work is based. In this form of therapy, work with the body, breath, habits, the unconscious, and interpersonal relations all focus on clearing up obstructions, preoccupations, and divisiveness in order to free one to experience the unity that underlies all apparent conflict within and without. The client learns to overcome discord, to reach beyond his limitations, and to experience an ever more encompassing unity, while at the same time maintaining his integrity as a conscious being. The therapist who himself has an appreciation of unitary consciousness will gradually help the client to let go of his absorption in each of the polarities of his life and thereby come closer to the experience of unity. In the process of therapy, identification with the ego is transcended and consciousness of the Self as the most comprehensive center of integration dawns.

Yoga therapy does not involve itself with any religion, the worship of any particular deity, or devotion to any religious or charismatic leader. It is an experimental and experiential quest, in which one gradually increases his capacity to be an unbiased observer. Its experiments are not limited by either the dogmatism of the mechanistic scientific paradigm or the dogmatism of religious belief. In this quest, one becomes a voyager within. There are maps and guides, but one must experience and find out for himself what is true and what is mere fancy or fantasy.

One's spiritual evolution takes place in three stages; the three highest chakras lead to progressively more encompassing experiences of spiritual unfoldment. At the first of these, the fifth chakra, *vishuddha*, the ego surrenders its authority to a universal nurturing center of love and wisdom. One remains identified with the more circumscribed ego, but the center of his interest is now some aspect of universal consciousness, which becomes the object of his devotion. At the sixth chakra, *ajna*, further detachment from the limited perspective of the ego takes place. One becomes a neutral observer of the melodramas of life, experiencing an underlying unity of being. Finally, at the seventh chakra, *sahasrara*, one passes beyond all involvement with form and realizes the highest state, nondual consciousness.

## SURRENDER

We have seen how the first three chakras draw one into the involutionary phase of the unfoldment of consciousness. One becomes entangled in the world of names and forms as he becomes addicted to the objects of his desires and then identifies with the ego and the scenarios the ego creates. The heart chakra is transitional, and the fifth chakra, vishuddha, brings the evolutionary phase of the journey into prominence.

At the stage of transition, the heart center, one leaves behind the distrust, desire, and pride of the lower three chakras and begins to experience a greater sense of unity with others. In the egoistic mode of consciousness, one remained focused on himself. He established the boundaries of and defended his territory, came to believe in his own capacities as an individual ego, and also became aware of his limitations as a separate person. Now at the anahata chakra, he experiences abundant love that radiates outward toward others. But we may wonder if it is possible to love genuinely and completely unless one has received such abundant love himself. To answer this question, we must climb still higher on the ladder of spiritual evolution to the vishuddha chakra. Here one finds the complementary experience to that which occurs at anahata. When one's heart is his center, he nurtures others; at vishuddha, the throat center, one receives nurturance.

At the anahata chakra, one gives up his egoistic preoccupations and, looking outward across the horizontal plane of his existence, becomes concerned with the needs of others. At vishuddha, one's outlook changes: at this center one looks upward toward that which transcends himself and humanity; he calls upward toward the heavens. While the heart center leads to the experience of humanism, the throat center awakens one to theism. At vishuddha, one gives up the ego as his center; he turns toward a more transcendent center and experiences the nurturance and guidance that flow from that center. He becomes enthralled with one or more of the glorious forms of God.

Educated people in modern society, for the most part, have not reached this perspective. They are functioning from the orientation of the egoistic or humanistic center. Modern psychology, with a few exceptions, does not appreciate the validity of the vishuddha perspective but considers the expressions of a person in this mode of consciousness to be an indication of regression to a more primitive mode of being. To the present-day societal establishment, the perspective of vishuddha seems irrational, mystical, other-worldly, impractical, naive, childlike, and irresponsible. Jung noted that "collectively we have not crossed the distance between anahata and vishuddha. So if one speaks of vishuddha, it is of course with a certain hesitation. We are stepping into the slippery future when we try to understand what that might mean. For in vishuddha we reach beyond our actual conception of the world, in a way we reach the ether region."[1]

In the vishuddha mode of consciousness, one recognizes the majesty and grandeur in all the manifest forms, from the colossal to the seemingly insignificant. He sees the archetypes that lie behind the world of names and forms as it is ordinarily experienced and becomes aware of divinity present in and sustaining all existence. Finding that he is loved and supported by the divine source from which all is manifest, he becomes like a trusting child and feels guided and protected. He experiences being fully accepted and forgiven, no matter what he has done or may do.

Devotional prayer, chanting, adoration of a divine form, and other devotional acts are means of surrendering one's absorption in his personality, desires, and egoistic concerns and turning toward the divine beloved. Becoming absorbed in the beloved instead of in his own desires or the cares and concerns of his ego, he begins to experience the limitless stream of love, compassion, and understanding that flows from the Mother or Father of this universe. He realizes that he is loved unconditionally and begins to accept himself unconditionally. Thus it is through experiencing divine love that one becomes truly able to love. The divine milk that is taken at the throat chakra flows through one's heart to nurture others. The great lovers of humanity have never felt that it is their love that is being expressed; they feel as though they are merely a conduit for the expression of divine love. They have succeeded in the most difficult of human undertakings: to surrender one's petty concerns and turn oneself over to that which is universal, to become a channel for the ever-flowing love that emanates from the fountainhead of life.

## Creativity

Physically, the throat serves the dual purpose of enabling one to take in sustenance and to express oneself. Although these may seem to be unrelated functions, they actually complement one another in forming the experience of the vishuddha chakra.

The voice is a vehicle through which we shape our experiences. By speaking in a derogatory or doubting manner, we can create negative experiences in ourselves and others, whereas by speaking loving words or chanting with devotion, we can create a heaven. In fact, the throat chakra is the center through which the individual creates his environment and his relationship to it; vishuddha is the center of creative expression in all forms.

One's creative abilities have the power to raise him to the heavens, but most people use their speech and creative powers in the service of the ego and the lower chakras. Modern works of art often lead both the creator and the experiencer to greater identification with worldly desires. Such use of our artistic capacity, instead of uplifting us, keeps us mired in the more primitive modes of consciousness. In the modern world, we have to a large extent lost our connection with the spiritual realm. Today, as Jung observed, "our conscious idea of God is abstract and remote, one hardly dares to speak of it; it has become taboo, or it is such a worn-out coin that one can hardly exchange it."[2]

Whether he is aware of it or not, one does not create through his ego alone. The ego has a severely limited scope of concern. Most creative artists describe their inspiration as coming from a more transcendent source; for one must surrender to a higher and more encompassing fountain of inspiration if he is to pour forth new insights or forms. The source from which guidance and inspiration flows to the artist has historically been called the muse; in the modern world, it is often called the unconscious. When another person experiences an inspired work of art, he also feels connected to that which transcends his egoistic focus. The vishuddha mode of experience may be summarized by the word "surrender"—not surrender to another person, to desires, to some cause or ism, but surrender to the divine. One surrenders to a higher power and only then does creative expression flow forth.

It is by directing his voice and creative powers upward that a human being establishes a relationship with divine forms. Chanting, prayer, and devotional art enable one to surrender his egoistic perspective and preoccupations and become aware of his connection to that which sustains him and the entire universe. Through surrendering one's egoistic concerns in devotional exercises, one brings his consciousness into relationship with the divine; he comes to feel that he is the child or beloved of that transcendent consciousness. Through this process, he opens himself to become aware of the divine nectar or ambrosia that has always been flowing to him and through him. He becomes aware that he is being looked after, guided, and loved by the supreme consciousness at all times, no matter how mischievous he may be, no matter how much he may at times ignore, turn away from, or deny that love.

From this center, one calls the divine down from the heavenly realm to nurture and sustain him. This mode of being has been evoked by the mystics throughout history. The

Psalms of the Old Testament convey this experience. They sing:

> The Lord is my shepherd; I shall not want.
> He maketh me to lie down in green pastures: he leadeth me
> beside the still waters.
> He restoreth my soul: he leadeth me in the paths of righteous-
> ness for his name's sake.
> Yea, though I walk through the valley of the shadow of death,
> I will fear no evil: for thou art with me; thy rod and thy staff
> they comfort me.
> Thou preparest a table before me in the presence of mine ene-
> mies: thou anointest my head with oil; my cup runneth over.
> Surely goodness and mercy shall follow me all the days of my
> life: and I will dwell in the house of the Lord forever.[3]

The vishuddha chakra is not only the center and source of creation within the individual; it is also the center through which one experiences the creative process in the macrocosm. When consciousness is centered here, one becomes aware of the primordial or archetypal forms and powers from which the universe is manifest. The truly great artists and spiritual leaders throughout history are those who have opened themselves to the experiences of those transcendent forms and have made the experiences available to others through their words and artistic expressions.

## Seeking Unconditional Love

The chakras depict the various motivations that a human being may have. Man is motivated by the survival instinct, the desire for sensory pleasure, mastery and power, and he is motivated to love and nurture others. But the attainment of all that one seeks in the first four modes of consciousness still leaves one incomplete and unfulfilled. More significant than any of those motivations is the desire to be loved and accepted unconditionally. If one experiences unconditional love and acceptance, all prior motivations lose their compelling quality.

Every client who comes to therapy feels he has been deprived of unconditional love and acceptance. Under the guise of attempting to resolve conflicts and problems, the client enters therapy to find unconditional love and acceptance in the therapeutic relationship. In the unique and artificial structure of psychotherapy, the therapist may provide a greater degree of unconditional acceptance than the client has been able to find anywhere else in his life. But every therapist has his human limitations. The therapist who is conscious of the vishuddha chakra may help the client to become aware of a more profound source of nurturance and love than even the therapist can provide. The following interchange with a young woman who had been experiencing insecurity and moments of panic is an example of a yoga therapist leading a client in this direction:

T: *As you were talking, I was imagining you in a place where everything that you needed was being provided. I wanted to say, "Don't panic; there is nothing to panic about. Everything you need is here; there is nothing for you to be afraid of." Then I imagined you experiencing all that you need being given to you. Whatever you needed in terms of nurturance, or comfort, or feeling good was given.*

C: *That feels real good. That is the way I felt the other morning in meditation, that I was really loved and cared for. Every time I think of that I just feel so warm. I don't have to be aggressively seeking it. It would be there if I just surrender.*

Throughout the course of history, human beings have directed their devotion toward a deity. They have worshiped God as Father or as Mother and have felt nurtured, guided, and accepted by that form of transcendent consciousness. Today, for many educated people, the belief in divinity is absent. One searches about like a homeless orphan for a refuge in the restless storm of modern life.

Life today is filled with interpersonal politics and competition. Many people have learned to be distrustful of others, of institutions, and of religious and secular leaders. Such a person develops an egoistic attitude, asserting, "I can take care of everything myself." He does not allow himself to relax and experience support and nurturance. He has not learned to acknowledge weakness, uncertainty, or vulnerability within himself and has yet to experience the comfort of surrendering his egoistic identifications.

The neck, an extremely vulnerable part of the body, is where the jugular vein is located. Certain species of animals expose their necks in play or in a fight as an indication of surrender. People who lack trust and are unable to experience surrender may complain of a tightness and constriction in the neck and throat. In our everyday parlance, a "stiff-necked" person is one who is stubborn, obstinate, and unyielding. Such a person may attempt to protect himself and hide his vulnerability. Rather than exposing his neck, he may wear stiff, tight-fitting collars, ties, or turtleneck shirts.

The yoga therapist may help the client to experience trust and vulnerability and to establish a connection to transcendent or ideal forms. He may guide the client in this direction without influencing him to adopt any particular religious belief. The following group therapy session illustrates this aspect of the therapeutic process:

C1: *I fight any kind of assistance or help from outside myself. I don't like to accept help from other people.*

T: *Are you saying that you have difficulty trusting another person or the group, that you stand by yourself rather than trusting?*

Cl: *I think that's part of it. (Crying) Last week I had some glimpses of being taken care of. Once in a class, you said something about divine nurturance, and I asked you what that was. You talked about being taken care of by the Divine Mother, but I couldn't really* understand. It wasn't something I could internalize or believe myself. It was something that I would have liked to believe, but I couldn't at the time.

I never had a clear concept of what God is. But last week after the group, I went home and lay down to sleep. I was thinking about my relationship with my husband and how I get to these points where I don't know what to do anymore. I surrendered myself to the Divine Mother. While I was doing it, I could hardly believe it. It was a revolutionary thing for me; I felt almost embarrassed even to myself. It didn't fit in with the way I was or the way I believe. It was such a good feeling for me to surrender like that, to feel as if some invisible person was holding me like I hold my son. It was such a powerful experience for me.

I've had trouble falling asleep after our weekly group meeting because so much comes out in the group. But that night I was able to fall asleep and sleep soundly all night. I've had a similar experience almost every night since. I feel embarrassed about telling you this; if I would tell my husband, he'd laugh at me and would think I was really kooky.

C2: This week I made a conscious effort to mentally picture myself being taken care of, just like I would take care of my child. I'd run the thought through my mind that I was whole and complete and cared for and loved by whatever God is. It's something I need to do.

C3: I can really identify with what you are both saying. A few weeks ago when I was home alone, I lay down and I was crying. There was a fear that I had gotten in touch with, and there was that feeling of not trusting; I had to be in control and to be tight and cautious and careful. Then I thought, "Who do I think I am? I can't control everything." If I would just trust and let go, just trust life. Not that I give up all responsibility: I do what I have to do, and at the same time, I'm aware that it's okay. Then I remembered an experience I had once in which I knew with my whole being that I would always be taken care of. I thought, "How could I go back to not trusting?" It's a very slow process. I know it all involves trust.

A person ordinarily expects his parents to be ideal rather than human. When his parents fail to live up to the ideal projected onto them, when they are not able to provide unconditional love, nurturance, and refuge from the travails of life, he may become cynical and untrusting. If he does not receive the love he seeks, he may blame himself and carry a sense of unworthiness and inadequacy into his adult years.

Clients in psychotherapy frequently report that they have tried unsuccessfully throughout their lives to gain acceptance from their parents. A client may come to the realization that he will never win his parents' approval, but that does not necessarily free him from feeling worthless. As long as he invests his parent with archetypal significance, considering his parent to be his basic source of love and acceptance, he will continue to feel unworthy and inadequate. However, if he is able to separate the archetype from the parent and find a more adequate expression of that archetype, his experience of being rejected can be replaced with the awareness that he is loved unconditionally.

In some instances, clients are made aware of this transference of the ideal onto a human being through direct confrontation, as is illustrated by the following dialogue:

C: *I was constantly rejected by my mother. I was never accepted. I can't remember ever being hugged by her when I was little or hearing the words, "I love you." I didn't get that from my father either.*

T: *What if I were to tell you something that will sound really absurd?*

C: *What's that?*

T: *That your father and mother aren't really your father and mother. That they don't really have the authority that you think they do.*

C: *Then I don't have anybody. Then I'm like an orphan; I'm lost and all alone.*

T: *Might you have another father and mother? (Pause) In telling you this, I'm sharing my own experience of how I relate to my parents.*

C: *How's that?*

T: *I don't experience them as really being my father and mother. They have shared with me what they have been able to share; they've taken care of me, guided me, and loved me the best they know how; but their understanding and their capacities are limited. I don't expect the unconditional love and acceptance I seek to come from them, but from another source.*

Another client described her response to a similar confrontation:

In our initial session together, I spent a lot of time complaining about my parents and other relatives. You told me that it is always frustrating to expect things from people that they simply aren't able to give. You said I might be better off looking toward my "real parents." I think you were talking about a supreme consciousness, a more complete and reliable source of nurturance and support. I realized that this change of focus could ultimately enhance my relationships with the loved ones I was complaining about. I'd need less from them. I'd be more capable of allowing them to be as they are.

That seemed like a terrific idea, but it was too big for me to deal with directly at the time, so I put it on the back burner to simmer. Now it seems to be spilling over into my life almost without effort and without my thinking about it. For example, often now when I'm angry, afraid, frustrated, or even simply bored, I don't stay very long in that frame of mind. I experience that there is a power I can call on so that I can do things in the world more smoothly than if I use my mind, ego, and emotions alone. I don't yet have a real understanding of what this power is or where it is, but I do know that I can use it.

The recognition of expressions of the parental archetypes other than one's natural parents does not depend on belief in a religion or belief in God in a particular form. But there is a shared assumption between client and therapist that some transcending, divinely nurturing force exists, and that if one opens oneself to that source, needs that cannot be adequately met in human relationships can indeed find fulfillment.

The source of nurturance can mistakenly be projected onto objects as well as people. Those objects that have accompanied the experience of being loved may themselves be sought out as though they could provide love and acceptance. For example, in childhood the experience of receiving unconditional love and acceptance is closely related to being fed. One unconsciously makes the connection even as an adult. Hence when one is anxious or fearful or feels inadequate or unloved, he may substitute physical nurturance for the love and acceptance he would like. In our society, many people overeat in order to eliminate the emptiness, hollowness, insecurity, or anxiety they experience when they do not feel loved and accepted. But food will not provide the comfort and security that one seeks. The following statement by an obese woman who had come to the United States from South America as a teenager describes the lack of nurturance she experienced upon coming here and the way in which she turned toward sweets to take the place of affection:

> I stayed in a house in the suburbs, and it was quiet all the time, just like a cemetery. Where I grew up, all the windows were open and you heard people talking. Merchants went around making loud noises, and there were always people in the house. Food was always cooking. But here I was isolated. It just felt dead to me. There were no trees and the homes all looked alike. The house where I lived was so cold and the kitchen was always so neat and clean. I just couldn't believe two white pieces of bread with a thin piece of bologna between was lunch. I was used to lots of rice and beans and tasty potatoes, a whole meal. I didn't feel fed at all. It wasn't just the food. I was starved for love and warmth. Somehow affection has gotten tied up with food. At home, I never had candy bars or cakes or

things like that. When I came to the United States, there were vending machines at school, which was strange to me—machines standing there all day and night. You put money in and a candy bar or some ice cream came out. I turned toward sweets.

In the course of therapy, this woman had become aware that her longing for sweets was a compensation for the nurturance she was not receiving from others. In a later therapy session, she realized that neither her parents nor food can provide the degree of nurturance and protection that she seeks, that she must turn toward a transcendent source to experience that sustenance.

C: *I was home alone and I wanted to forget about my problems and enjoy eating. I let myself act out my feelings to see what it is that I'm so attached to. My first reaction was that the food was security. I wanted to be held by the orange. I could see how silly it was.*

T: *Don't you find that kind of nurturance apart from food?*

C: *I don't recall being held by my mother. Sometimes even now when I go to visit my parents, I would like to kiss and hug them, but instead we sit and enjoy my mother's food. I'm looking for something more than food and kissing and hugging. When I kiss a couple of times, it gives me joy, but then I become tired of it.*

T: *How can you maintain that feeling?*

C: *I don't know. I think that food is going to give it to me, and it does for the first few moments, but then comes the depression.*

T: *Could that urge be satisfied by turning to some spiritual object?*

C: *Yes; once instead of eating, I called for God's help. Then I started crying and just let it out. I don't know why I was crying.*

T: *I wonder if it would help even more to visualize God nurturing and loving you.*

C: *Is there a female God?*

T: *In the Christian tradition, there is Mary, Christ's mother. In some Eastern traditions, she is called the Divine Mother.*

C: *You know, when I call "Mother" when I'm feeling pain, I'm not actually calling for my mother, for her as a person. Usually I feel relieved and cry.*

In the vishuddha mode of consciousness, one experiences in a theistic way; he experiences relationships to ideal forms. If he does not find an adequate carrier for his ideal, he projects the ideal onto people, institutions, and objects and eventually experiences disappointment. The therapist's function here is to help the client find adequate symbols through which he can establish his relationship to the ideal forms. In some cases, leading the client to a relationship with symbolic expressions found within spiritual traditions serves that purpose.

Many psychologists would react negatively to this viewpoint, arguing that the therapist is encouraging the client to substitute benign fantasies for the "hard reality of life." Reductionist therapies do not offer the possibility that the longed-for relationship can be fulfilled. The sought-after love and acceptance is interpreted as a primitive wish fulfillment that does not square with the reality of the adult world. According to this view, maturity comes when one gives up the wish for unconditional acceptance and understanding.

By contrast, yoga therapy, as well as other therapies that acknowledge the archetypal level of human experience, offers the possibility of establishing a relationship with the ideal nurturing parent and with other ideals. In these therapies, one learns to respect his need for unconditional love and acceptance and develops a conscious relationship to those symbols and forms that embody the archetypes of the nurturing parent. One is encouraged to withdraw his projections from objects, people, and institutions and to direct his longing toward symbols and forms that can adequately express the archetype without leading to disappointment.

In the course of yoga therapy, one learns that even the ideal forms, which may be experienced as divinities existing outside oneself, are really projections of one's inner being. Ultimately, this process leads to the experience of a transcendent core within oneself. As one progresses in spiritual awareness, he is encouraged to realize that the source of nurturance and acceptance is not external but is at the center of one's being. This is perhaps the most important contribution of meditation and the Eastern spiritual traditions. As the following client indicates, this realization may be difficult for those who are taught to believe in a god that is forever external to oneself:

C: *It sometimes scares me to believe in divinity within myself. It is so different from what I am used to.*

T: *What are you used to?*

C: *The notion that God is out there and we are here in misery. He is there to help us when we need help, but the only things that we have are the things that are down here. These are in our domain, and God is out there somewhere. The challenge of this new perspective seems to bring me more to life: I am not depending on God out there to take care of me or to give me paradise. I can take responsibility for the spirituality also. In the old way, we could take care of the physical aspect, and the emotional was ours too; but once you got to the spiritual, that was always left to God.*

Another client expressed a growing awareness of a transcendent center of consciousness within:

You are the first therapist that I have come to not just for psychological or emotional problems, but to deal with spiritual concerns as well. Somehow I connect religion with my old experience of God as being someone outside of me. In order to learn about God, I had to learn it from other people. And they taught that He was out there and up there, and the only way to get there was to go through them. My experience in the past few years is that God is within; the way to understand God is to understand myself and to go within. When I have meditated with that attitude, it works.

In psychotherapy the client may develop a positive transference, projecting the archetype of divine nurturance onto the therapist. Some therapists, in order to raise their own sense of worth and esteem or to manipulate the client, may encourage such transference reactions rather than encouraging the client to relate to the archetype through spiritual symbols or forms or to experience the archetype within himself. Such encouragement leads the client to become dependent on the therapist and eventually to become disappointed. The following description by a client of her relationship with her former therapist illustrates the way that the archetype of the nurturing, all-accepting parent may be projected onto the therapist with the therapist's encouragement. The client then expects the therapist to extend that relationship into his personal life outside of the therapy session. Disappointment, frustration, and anger are the inevitable results.

In Dr. K's presence, I felt protection and care, but even more. Through him, I had a sense that not only was I provided for and loved, but also all things were watched over and taken care of. The amphetamines and antidepressants that I had previously required to fight my despondency were no longer needed. I felt happy and alive again. Through this doctor, I felt reconnected to the source of life from which I had been cut off.

I began to mistake his kindness and concern as a personal response to me. The desire for union became very intense. I longed for us to be together and fervently believed it would be so. I associated with him all the childhood dreams that a young girl formulates and still carries around with her as an adult. I projected all those hopes onto him, conceiving of a life of relative simplicity, shared with him in love and reverence.

When the unreality of my dreams hit me, I suffered an unendurable sense of loss. I experienced tremendous grief and pain; I felt totally abandoned and alone. It was not that a certain kind of love and caring didn't still exist, for it did; but it was not directed toward me in the very special way I had imagined. I felt only the absence of all I had hoped for and lived for. Along with the pain, there was anger too, directed toward this doctor who had let me misdirect myself so completely and for so long. I felt I should not have been allowed to make that error and that he could have prevented it.

This client terminated therapy and later entered a more spiritually oriented therapeutic process. During the course of that therapy, she withdrew that which she had been projecting onto her first therapist and came to experience a more fulfilling center of nurturance within herself.

When the sense of protection was withdrawn from the person whom I depended upon for it, it slowly emerged from sources within. I had definite, clear experiences where I felt led, directed, and guided from deep within. Gradually, the feeling of protection and guidance became more constant, and I felt wholly enveloped by loving care. As I felt this love and care more, I also found myself more loving and caring. My whole life changed.

One may also project the archetype of the ideal nurturing parent onto one's mate, as the following excerpt from a therapy session illustrates. In this session, the therapist helps the client to become aware that what she is seeking outside is really to be found within herself.

C: *Ever since my teens, I have been preoccupied with a fantasy somewhat like the story of Cinderella. The charming prince comes and takes care of me. He is powerful and he gives me a sense of worth by caring for me. He is supposed to be perfect. My husband had some of the qualities I was looking for, but I augmented the whole thing, making a perfect being out of him in my mind. I saw my husband as some type of savior. I had the illusion that once we were married, there would be happiness forever. But after we had our daughter, he started to have some psychological difficulties himself. That really shocked me. I wasn't ready to have my Prince Charming have any psychological problems.*

T: *It seems that the sense of worth in your fantasy doesn't belong to you, that you see it as being out there. The prince has all the self-worth and he can dispense it. Where is Prince Charming getting his power?*

C: *He has it. He is all-powerful.*

T: *And you are just recognizing it in him, you are just recognizing what is already there?*

C: *Yes.*

T: *And your husband lost his power?*

C: *(Pause) I guess he never had it. I put it there in my fantasy.*

T: *So the power and sense of self-worth belong to you, and you give it to Prince Charming in your fantasy so that he can give it back to you?*

An executive in his early forties gave the following account of his therapy:

Last year I saw a conventional therapist for about six months. That process seemed to have a circularity and opaque-

ness that failed to yield any insights that I considered significant. My motivation for going was the conflicts I was having
with my parents. I came out of that therapy experience without understanding the real nature of my contribution to that
conflict. I was determined to find a new psychotherapist who
combined psychology with spiritual practice, knowledge, and
insight.

I had been intently seeking acceptance in the outer world.
I wanted desperately to please my wife all the time, to have
her never become angry at me, and I wanted to feel that my
parents love and accept me. This search drove me to try to
find ways to meet their conditions.

After I described a conflict I had with my wife last week,
you asked if I felt she accepted me without any conditions.
Clearly not; there were definite conditions. Then you asked a
question that triggered dramatic personal insights: "Is there
anybody who accepts you unconditionally?" I thought.
Certainly my wife loves me deeply, and yet sometimes she
places conditions on her acceptance of me. Family? Each parent definitely has expectations of me and does not fully accept
me unless the expectations are met. Friends? Same thing.
Myself? Do I accept myself unconditionally? Definitely not.
My mind is the least accepting of all. It has an endless string
of conditions for accepting me. I work hard to meet one, and
before I've finished, five more conditions jump into my consciousness.

You asked again, "Is there anybody who accepts you
unconditionally?" Then I felt a wave of emotion sweep
through me. The Supreme accepts me unconditionally. I felt
unconditional acceptance flood through my heart. The
awareness flowed as direct feeling, no longer as a mental idea.
For so long, I had sought unconditional acceptance in the
outer world—from friends, family, job, my own mind.
Whenever conditions arose, I tried hard to meet them. But I
never experienced unconditional acceptance.

I realized then that the drawing force of my life is a continual search for unconditional love and acceptance. I am a
seeker of unconditional love, and I can receive it only from

the inner world—from the Supreme. All I have to do is open myself to it, and the feeling flows into my awareness—because it's already there. There is no way I can ever get unconditional acceptance from anything in the outer world or from my mind, with all its confusions. Only the Supreme can give this unalloyed love. For me to focus my seeking on my wife or parents rather than on the Supreme is to place an impossible burden on them. It's unfair. And yet for all my life, that's exactly what I had been doing. Now I feel like my life is permanently centered. And my need to look for this unconditional acceptance from others and from my mind is much less.

In my relationship with my wife, there have been no recurrences of our past conflicts. I can accept her non-acceptance of me when it occurs. I acknowledge to myself at such times that the Supreme loves me unconditionally, that I can't expect my wife to, and that it's okay.

When one experiences such a relationship with the transcendent, he no longer relates to others in terms of demands that he be loved and accepted, for that fundamental need is already being fulfilled. He can relate more fully and spontaneously to another person without distorting his experience of that person because of his own needs. That enables him to become more responsive to others.

Transference may extend beyond one's relationship to parents, mate, or therapist. A person may idealize a movie star, musician, hero, political, religious, or cult leader, or any figure portrayed as an ideal, and direct his devotional feelings toward that person. Or he may surrender to a political, religious, or cult movement with similar zeal. If he becomes enraptured with an ideal as it is projected onto the worldly sphere, he may go to any lengths for that ideal. He may become caught up in intensely melodramatic experiences in sacrificing himself for a cause rather than establishing objectivity to observe the grand archetypal themes being played out around him. Far too late, he is likely to find that his idol or cause is not all that he or it claimed to be.

If one's devotion is directed toward a cause, he may find guidance and nurturance from that movement and surrender his decision making, his responsibility, his territoriality, even his possessions, to the cause or its leader. It is important to distinguish surrender to a form that claims to be an ideal from surrender to that which genuinely symbolizes the ideal. Many people are so eager to find support or parental figures that they surrender themselves to a leader or institution that they believe will rescue them from their unhappiness. They are prepared to follow almost any charismatic figure. Such people are merely surrendering to the ego of another and are ready to believe any nonsense that may be put forth by the leader or institution.

One of the most important qualities to be developed in yoga therapy is discrimination *(viveka)*, the ability to distinguish between that which is unreal, insubstantial, and illusory, and that which is real, substantial, and abiding. The world contains many allurements and attractions that promise one fulfillment but that ultimately lead to disappointment if one surrenders to them. One must learn to distinguish between those allurements and that which stands behind and manifests the alluring forms that enrapture human beings.

As a person evolves, his experience of surrender also evolves. Surrender is initially linked with experiences at the more primitive chakras: a person may surrender in a battle for survival and be slain; one may surrender to a person or object that gives him sensory gratification; he may devote himself to someone who has more power and authority than he—he may identify with the person or institution to which he is surrendering and thereby feel a greater sense of power himself. All these forms of surrender are adumbrations: they prefigure surrender to a state of consciousness that transcends the ego's subject-object mode of being. Ultimately, one must learn to surrender egoistic consciousness to a mode of consciousness that is far more comprehensive. That is the experience of the vishuddha chakra. One must be careful not to stop short by merely surrendering to a cause or to the ego of another. It is at the throat chakra that one also experiences romance; the romances of ancient and modern times are expressions of this mode of consciousness. As Cervantes' Don Quixote shows us time and again, anyone or anything can become the object of one's romantic inclinations. If the object later turns out to be unworthy of one's investment, he will become disillusioned, but the longing for romance will not cease. For one's unrelenting quest is to find an object that is not merely a receptacle for his projected ideal but actually is that ideal. One need not create romances out of fantasy. If he simply empties himself of all imagined romances, he will find that there is a substratum to life that is the basis and the fulfillment of all romances—a realm more alluring, majestic, and splendorous than he could ever envision in fantasy. All romances conjured up by the human imagination are merely adumbrations, imperfect imitations, that point the way to a realm where fulfillment of one's ideals can be experienced.

## Yantra

When one is unaware of the archetypal level of his being, he unknowingly acts out archetypal themes. He is not free to choose his own attitudes and actions. At the vishuddha chakra, one becomes conscious of the various archetypes; he learns to appreciate the majesty that under-lies even the most ordinary occurrences. To the extent that he is able to remain a neutral observer of the archetypal enactments, he also becomes free from the power and dom-inance of the archetypes.

Yoga assists one in becoming aware of the archetypes as they function in his life and in freeing himself from their dominance over him. Each yogic practice, from the hatha yoga postures to the use of mantra in meditation, helps one to become aware of the archetypal themes being played out in the dramas of everyday life. In yoga therapy, one may come to know the hero, the wise old man, the Divine Mother, the fool, the trickster, or numerous other ideal forms. He becomes aware of the archetypes within himself as well as in others, and of the dramas that evolve from them. He learns how his identification with a particular archetypal expression restricts his awareness and freedom, and gradually transcends identification with each archetype and its limitations in order to experience all his possibilities. The yoga therapist may use dreams or artistic expression to help the client become aware of the ideal forms. He may also ask the client to concentrate on a particular form that symbolizes a divine state of being in order that the client may align his consciousness with that transcendent state of consciousness.

Both Sankhya and tantra psychology, upon which much of yoga therapy is based, lead one to an awareness of underlying archetypal principles from which the phenomenal universe is manifest. Sankhya is based on the science of numbers, and according to this science, each number symbolizes a mode of experience. For example, the number two represents polarity and all experiences of a dualistic nature, while the number three introduces a new perspective that comprehends polarity. Sankhya describes the many psychological, philosophical, and practical meanings and implications of each number. The science of yantra is a branch of tantra that is concerned with geometric archetypal forms—the point, line, circle, triangle, square, and so on—which are the basic building blocks of the phenomenal universe. In tantric practices, one gains mastery over the archetypal forms and thus mastery over the manifest world.

In yoga meditation, most students concentrate on a sound form called a *mantra*. As the student's ability to focus the mind is strengthened, he may also be given a *yantra* or visual form upon which to focus his attention during meditation. A mantra is the expression of the ideal in the realm of sound, whereas a yantra is its expression in the visual realm.

A yantra is a particular type of mandala used in the yogic tradition. It is made up of basic geometric forms arranged in a prescribed manner. The yantra usually has a central point *(bindu)* around which triangles, circles, squares, and other shapes are ordered. The prescribed arrangement is a symbolic depiction that elicits the experience of a particular archetypal mode of consciousness. The arrangement reflects an underlying order within the psyche and the underlying organization of some facet of the universe. A yantra is a kind of mathematical formula expressing basic laws of the universe, similar to an equation like $E=mc^2$, but using geometric forms rather than numbers or letters as the means of expression. The yantra expresses a very high order of unity and integration and is also the expression or embodiment of an extremely evolved state of consciousness. The yogic practitioner may focus his attention on a particular yantra for many minutes each day in order to experience its nature and significance. He may gaze at the form or sit with the eyes closed, visualizing the form within.

Jung was very interested in the use of visual images in psychotherapy and frequently had his patients draw or paint visual representations of their emotional and psychological states. Typically, the painting would reflect the patient's inner turmoil and discord. But some paintings produced by patients were remarkably similar to mandalas or yantras of the Eastern meditative traditions. Jung noted the similarity, concluding that the more harmonious forms were produced by patients as the more integrative aspects of their unconscious came forward. To the degree that a patient was in touch with the deeper levels of integration within, forms similar to the Eastern mandalas and yantras spontaneously appeared in his artistic expressions.

**Yantra of the Anahata Chakra**

Further comparison of the way that mandalas are used in Eastern meditative traditions and in Western psychotherapy leads one to become aware of a striking contrast between the methodologies of most Western therapies and the process of self-transformation in yoga. In analytic therapy, forms are analyzed as representations of one's inner state. Mandalas are considered to be expressions that arise from the unconscious and that betoken a rearranging of the personality and a new centering. It is the exceptional client who is able to bring forth these forms that express order, balance, and wholeness. Contrastively, the Eastern methodologies "anticipate the natural course of development and substitute for the spontaneous production of symbols a deliberately selected set of symbols prescribed by tradition."[4] In the yogic tradition a yantra or mantra is *given* to the student as an object of concentration. The student is asked to spend considerable time each day concentrating on the integrative form of the mantra or yantra. He is taught not to be swayed by the many distractions the mind produces but to center his consciousness ever more completely on the unifying form of the mantra or yantra. He has simply to still himself rather than wandering about in his thoughts, fantasies, daydreams, and remembrances. In order to focus his mind on the ideal form, he must withdraw his attention from the conflicts, disharmonies, and melodramas of his life. During the periods of focused awareness, he identifies with the archetypal form of the mantra or yantra. As the process is repeated each day, the old preoccupations of his mind are increasingly replaced with the divine form of his object of concentration. In this way the object of concentration leads him to an ever more complete awareness of the underlying order of his psyche and to a more universal mode of consciousness.

Modern therapies, for the most part, do not have comparable methods that draw one toward highly evolved states of consciousness.* In modern therapy, one gropes and meanders along the path leading to self-understanding, but in the yogic tradition one is pulled toward the goal with the aid of the evolved forms. One increasingly lets go of his identification with his personality and worldly melodramas and embodies and expresses the unifying order of the universal form in accordance with which he is shaping his mind. Through repeated concentration on the given form, his old discords are gradually left behind and are replaced with the harmonious form of the mantra or yantra.

---

* Exceptions are found in psychosynthesis, which is derived from yoga philosophy, and in other schools of psychotherapy that use guided visualization techniques to help clients experience archetypal expressions. In these therapies the client may be asked to visualize a wise old man, a source of radiant light, or some other ideal form and to receive guidance or nurturance from that archetypal form. However, such techniques lead to only a dim recognition of the archetypes.

Jung understood the value of using such forms in this way. He wrote that he was "in complete agreement with the Eastern view, [that] the mandala is not only a means of expression but also produces an effect. . . . Through the ritual action, attention and interest are led back to the inner, sacred precinct, which is the source and goal of the psyche and contains the unity of life and consciousness."[5]

In analytic psychology, there is also a movement toward integration and unity, although final integration is never achieved. The mandalas drawn by patients never fully reach the degree of integration achieved in the Eastern mandalas. In summarizing Jung's view, his close student Jolande Jacobe wrote:

> The mandalas with their mathematical structure are pictures, as it were, of the "primal order of the total psyche," and their purpose is to transform chaos into cosmos. For these figures not only express order, they also bring it about.
>
> Meditation on Yantra images . . . aims precisely at the creation of an intrapsychic order in the meditator. Naturally the mandalas of analysands can never achieve the artistic perfection and finish, the "traditionally established harmony," of the mandalas of the East, which are not spontaneous products of the psyche but works of conscious artistry. We have cited them only as parallels in order to show that they rest on the same psychic foundations and therefore disclose striking similarities.[6]

In yoga therapy, concentration on a mantra or yantra outside of the therapy session may be integrated with an exploration of the unconscious within the session. These are not exclusive processes but can complement one another in the growth process. Concentration on a mantra or yantra helps to lead consciousness in a particular direction, while the exploration of the mental contents in therapy can help to clear up the involvements that keep one absorbed in the world drama and unable to fully concentrate on the ideal form.

Yantras and mantras may also be used to help one deal with unresolved issues related to a particular chakra. Each chakra has a unique yantra and a particular mantra that are the visual and sound symbols of that chakra. One may concentrate on the symbol of a particular chakra or on the physical location in the body that corresponds to that chakra. Such concentration helps to bring one's consciousness into that field of expression. As a result, one's involvement with a particular archetype may become intensified. Regular meetings with a yoga teacher or therapist are often helpful in enabling one to deal effectively with the unconscious material that surfaces as a result of such exercises.

### Beyond Archetypes

If one is fortunate enough to penetrate behind the veil of materiality and to know the subtle majestic ideals from which the world of form is fashioned, he encounters another danger: he must be careful not to become enraptured even by the ideal forms. Attachment to archetypes can hold one back from still greater vistas, and identification with an archetype can lead one to lose his stability. It is important to maintain a neutral center of consciousness in order to experience the archetypes without being taken over by them. Here one needs the aid of a still more evolved mode of consciousness.

Jung and his followers developed a psychology based on the vishuddha mode of experience. In Jung's psychology, the ideals are regarded as existing within the psyche. Jung explored the realm of vishuddha in depth throughout the course of his life, and he left valuable maps and charts describing this realm that is so foreign to ego-consciousness. Few modern psychologists have reached this heightened understanding of the psyche. Nevertheless, Jung's psychology is limited, for he did not enter into the realms that lie beyond vishuddha. Jung repeatedly criticized Freud for his reductionism, for Freud understood the realms of the higher chakras in terms of the primitive chakras. Yet Jung's psychology may also be considered reductive, though not nearly to the degree of

psychoanalytic psychology. Jung elevated psychological phe-
nomena, for he interpreted the lower realms in terms of the
mode of experience found at vishuddha. He nevertheless
understood still more evolved modes of consciousness and
interpreted more comprehensive realms in terms of this fifth
chakra rather than appreciating them in their own right. This
mode of consciousness is a rung on the ladder of evolution,
but it is not the final step, for it is still a dualistic mode of consciousness. There is a subject and an object that is
experienced—for instance, a devotee and an object of devotion—whether that object is gross or subtle, whether it is
experienced as being outside or within oneself.

Archetypal forms lead one to the experience of majestic,
transcendent ideals from which the world of the senses is
formed, but ultimately one goes beyond involvement with all
forms and becomes aware of that source from which they are
manifest. Before unitary consciousness can be fully experienced one must take two more steps beyond vishuddha. Yoga
psychology goes on to explore those modes of experience
found above the realm of archetypes.

## SELF-OBSERVATION

At the ajna chakra, the sixth mode of consciousness,
located between the eyebrows, one gains distance from the
archetypes and from the dramas created in the other chakras.
One becomes the objective observer, the witness who does
not identify with the world of names and forms. One whose
consciousness is fully absorbed in this realm may be called a
seer, a sage, a visionary. His understanding reaches beyond
ordinary intellectual knowledge, for he sees into the subtleties
of the hidden laws and principles of the universe. At vishuddha the subtle principles are experienced as symbolic forms,
but at the ajna chakra one attains a still greater power of
understanding that goes beyond those forms. The Sanskrit
word *ajna* means "the lotus of command." Here one has com-

mand over the phenomenal universe. According to the yogic tradition, all knowledge can be found within, through absorption in the ajna chakra.

As a result of the awakening to this mode of consciousness, some people may experience psychic powers. If this happens while the egoistic mode of consciousness is predominant in the personality, one will use such insight for his own aggrandizement. Others may experience this mode of consciousness in a partial and distorted way, for one may be intellectual and detached from the emotional involvement generated at the lower chakras without having attained clarity of understanding. The intellectual remains absorbed in the illusory problems and conflicts of the world. Jung said of modern man: "Our ajna is caught in this world. It is a spark of light, imprisoned in the world, and when we think, we are thinking in terms of the world."[7]

For most people, the ajna mode of consciousness is used in the service of a less evolved sphere. For example, one may use his intellect to avoid a disaster, to attain something he desires, to prove his self-worth, to criticize, or to compete with or manipulate another person. Many people who are caught up in the third chakra struggle to prove their adequacy through intellectual accomplishments or through amassing a great deal of information. A person who feels vulnerable and of low self-worth may attempt to cover over his experience of inadequacy with his intellectualizations. Rarely will such a person be able to see beyond his intellectual preoccupations; he will be bound to his worldly concerns and thus will not penetrate to the source of wisdom and understanding. To reach that source, one must cease to identify with the mind and its thoughts and develop the ability to witness the mind. One must become a quiet, still observer rather than being swept along in the intellectual process.

From the perspective of yoga psychology, consciousness is not an attribute of the mind; rather, the mind is an instrument of consciousness. As long as one identifies with the mind, his consciousness seems to take on the limitations of that instrument. If one further identifies with the thoughts that run through the mind, consciousness becomes even more constricted. In order for the unrealized potentials of consciousness to become evident, consciousness must disengage from its instrument and the contents of that instrument.

One can use a computer to accomplish astounding feats of information storage and computation, but the computer has obvious limitations. It can take in only certain kinds of information; its structure and the programs that direct it allow it to calculate only in certain ways. The mind is useful for experiencing and dealing with the phenomenal world, but it too has limitations. It is limited by the way it receives information, the range of information it can receive, and the way it processes that which it receives. There are limitations that are imposed by one's "programs" or habits of reasoning, and limitations of the instrument itself. For example, the mind is incapable of calculating with the speed of a modern computer.

Just as a computer can be turned off or unplugged, so too the mind can be stilled. Most people imagine that when the mind is stilled, nothing occurs for the individual; they imagine that the state of mental stillness is one of unconsciousness, deep sleep, or death. But advanced practitioners of yoga who have learned to turn off the mind report a quite different occurrence. Instead of going to a state of unconsciousness, they experience a vastly expanded consciousness that is not encumbered by the instrument called mind and its contents.

Meditation is the means of disengaging from the mind and its contents, thereby enabling one to experience alternate modes of consciousness. Through meditation one can cease identifying with thoughts, emotions, and desires, and the tendencies toward action that arise out of those thoughts and desires. Meditation is also a means of ceasing to identify with one's past and with the melodramas of life that arise out of the lower chakras. Meditation helps one learn to live more fully and spontaneously in the present rather than being so completely encumbered by the programs and memories that reside in the unconscious mind. Meditation and the application of its principles in the conduct of one's life are central to yoga therapy.

In yoga meditation, one is given a mantra on which to concentrate his mind. Holding the same thought in the mind over a considerable period of time helps to disengage the mind from the thinking process, from the subject-object mode of experience, and from sequential or cause/effect reasoning. If one's concentration is interrupted by the unfinished business of the mind—memories, desires, daydreams, discomforts, fears, expectations, and so on—the tendency is to become absorbed in the melodramas that result from those mental perturbations. But the meditator learns to remain a witness, to neutrally observe the activities taking place in his mind. To the extent that he is successful in the endeavor, he frees himself from the conflict, dissatisfaction, and unrest that ordinarily result from mental turmoil.

Meditation is a means of letting go of one's preoccupations and complexes and living more fully in the present. The meditator's increased ability to focus his attention on the intended object carries over to his life in the external world. He becomes better able to concentrate on the task at hand without distraction, emotionalism, and daydreaming. As a result of regular periods of meditation, one becomes more effective in carrying out the tasks of everyday life.

In psychoanalysis and related psychotherapies, one's personal history is considered to be weighty and significant. One spends many arduous hours rooting through complexes, conflicts, and entanglements in order to disengage from distortions that he has been superimposing on his current life situation. As he recalls experiences from the past, he scrutinizes them carefully in order to understand them more objectively. He takes his story to be very serious indeed. One client told me:

I've been frustrated in previous therapies I've been in because of the limited goal. Finding out about the unconscious and whatever has been repressed is blown out of proportion. That has never been satisfying to me. It's so seducing that you get lost in bringing it out, as if that were the thing to work for and there was nothing else beyond that, beyond what we call the person, conscious and unconscious.

In yoga psychology, one's personal history is considered to be relatively superficial—a cover for one's true identity. From the very beginning, one learns not to identify with his past, for it is not considered necessary to scrutinize one's life history in order to lessen its effect in the present. Complexes that have resulted from past experiences are worked out in one's present interactions without focusing so extensively on their causes. One may explore the way the past has led to his present problems, but finding causal links is secondary to dealing with current conflicts. Part of the client's problem is that he already takes his personal history too seriously, identifying with his story and ignoring his true Self. In the course of yoga therapy, the therapist will help the client to gain a more detached, objective, and neutral view of his past and to appreciate aspects of himself that transcend his personal history. He will not lead the client toward a causal explanation or historical rationale for his current way of being but will instead focus on modifying the client's way of being in the present.

Meditation is the yogic technique for dissolving one's identification with his personal history. In meditation, one learns to neutrally observe his thoughts, memories, emotions, and desires. Ordinarily, one identifies with his thoughts, and a thought with which one identifies then leads to desire and finally to behavior. One acts out the thought, and a scenario develops. Beginning with a single thought, an entire drama is created. But in meditation, one becomes a detached witness to the spectacle taking place in his mind and personality. When a thought arises in the mind during meditation, the meditator learns to observe the thought disinterestedly. Without personal involvement, the thought cannot lead to desire, action, and a consequent scenario. As one learns to watch each thought without judgment, evaluation, interest, or aversion, he becomes free from any compelling quality that the thought might otherwise have over him.

Clients in yoga therapy are encouraged to meditate daily outside of the therapy session, but half an hour to an hour of meditation each day will not in itself lead to the resolution of one's problems. It may lead to some degree of objectivity and neutrality in confronting the turmoil going on within and without, but one may still feel overwhelmed by the ever-new conflicts, predicaments, and disappointments that arise in the course of each day. A small island of calm may sometimes be reached during meditation, but afterwards one soon becomes swept up in the frantic activity of modern life and loses awareness of that calm center within. In order to progress further toward peace and equanimity, one must also learn to deal with the thoughts, sensations, and external demands that occur as one acts in daily life. Therefore, one must learn to practice meditation in action. In this practice, one applies exactly the same principles that are used in meditation: he observes his thoughts and desires rather than identifying with them. He also witnesses his mental and emotional responses to external stimuli and demands.

The following excerpts from a series of group therapy sessions highlight the development of a neutral, observing attitude toward thoughts and emotions. The sessions from which these excerpts are taken occurred approximately eight months after the start of weekly group meetings. In the first excerpt, the client becomes aware of her tendency to analyze and pass judgment on her thoughts:

> During the week, a little thing that someone would say would set a whole cycle of thoughts and emotions going in me. I was interested in watching this process. At times, I would

find myself wanting to analyze my experiences. I'd ask myself, Why do you feel this way? Or I'd think, I know what's happening here. But it would just complicate the experience. The more I tried to figure out, the more I would get emotionally involved with the thought or feeling.

Most of the time I'm passing judgment on what I'm thinking or feeling, analyzing it or having some kind of mental reaction to the thought or feeling. This reaction creates more thoughts; it seems to generate a whole new scenario to be replayed. But neutrally observing my thoughts doesn't generate any new thoughts; it settles me down.

It's not easy for me to watch my thoughts and emotions. I find it's nearly impossible for me not to have some kind of judgment on what I'm thinking or feeling. There's almost a constant stream of judging of whether it's right or wrong. And as soon as a judgment is passed, there's an additional thing to deal with. Passing a judgment seems to create a whole new flood of thoughts. For instance, if I believe I'm thinking something good, then there's usually a whole barrage of thoughts that generates a feeling of pride.

Sometimes I'll be lying in bed and thoughts will be coming. I'll see myself beginning to get attached to the thoughts or involved with them. Then I'll remind myself, Don't get attached; just look at them, watch them.

In a later session, this client further described her increasing awareness of how she ordinarily reacts to thoughts and how these reactions lead to an intensification of emotions:

I woke up in the middle of the night. It was two in the morning, and the thought was in my head, What if someone got into the apartment? Then I reacted to that thought. I started to tighten up and I could feel my heart pumping faster. Then came different thoughts. I was remembering something I had read about a rapist breaking into a house and chopping off his victim's arms. Then I started to feel angry and my stomach began to knot up. All these emotions came. Ordinarily, if I didn't watch the process, I would get real caught up in the emotions.

There's a constant stream of thoughts in my head. Most of the time, it seems like a vicious cycle. I have thoughts and react to them; this brings more thoughts and I react to them, too—like the thought that someone is in the apartment. I'm in the habit of reacting to that thought with fear, and that leads to further scary thoughts, and I react to those with more fear. I find myself wondering how it would be to let all the thoughts go and not react to them.

As therapy progressed, this client began to discriminate more clearly between her emotions and the witnessing consciousness. She also became aware that in order to give up her identification with "negative" thoughts and emotions, she would have to give up her identification with those thoughts that she considered to be "positive" as well.

This week I was observing emotions in myself rather than identifying with them. I would notice anger, anxiety, fear—the things I consider to be negative. I would notice those things, but I'd disidentify with them. I would say, That's Sue. See how she's so fearful. See how she's so caught up and worried. But I am just a neutral observer. I would find myself observing and saying to myself, See how involved she is in being angry, and Did you notice how she . . . ? Of course, a lot of times I would just be caught up in what I considered to be negative emotions, but as soon as I became aware of them, I would stop identifying with those emotions. I would observe the anger, the anxiety, or the frustration, and I would say, I'm not that anxiety; I'm not that fear.

After I did that for a few days, I was watching my children as they were going to school. I thought, They're such nice kids; I just love them so much. And it dawned on me that if I wasn't the negative emotions, then I wasn't the positive emotions either. That was kind of a shock to me. That wasn't as easy as saying, I'm not anger; I'm not proud or depressed. I thought, If I'm not the negative things, I'm not the positive things either. I began thinking, You can't be one without the other; the opposites come together like a set. You're going to have to be both of them or neither. If you're not a hater, then you're not a lover; and if you're not impatient, then you're not patient either. You can't be one without the other.

It was a funny feeling because I've always wanted to be rid of all those things that I consider negative, but I always wanted the positive things to increase. Later, I watched myself feel that I was very kind or friendly to someone. I would say to myself, I'm not that friendliness; I'm not that kindness. Everything that went through my mind, I would say that I wasn't that. I must be something that's removed from all those things, but I don't yet know what it is.

In the following weeks, she also began to watch her emotional reactions to other family members. The skill that she was developing in being a witness to her emotions and thoughts helped her to remain centered and to cope more effectively with situations that previously had led to emotional conflicts. The following excerpt from a group session illustrates this point:

C2 (another member of the group): I used to deny a lot of the emotions that I considered negative, like anger and jealousy. I'm more aware of them now. But going around expressing the anger seems to be as much of a trap as denying it.

T: Could you accept and experience those emotions without acting them out and without identifying with them?

C1: (Sue): When I feel angry with my kids, sometimes I show it—I yell! If they're fighting, I'll feel myself getting angry and I'll scream, "You kids are always yelling at one another! I'm sick of everybody around here fighting!" That gets everybody around me going. Suddenly my husband is mad, the kids are mad, and the dog hides 'cause she's frightened when anyone yells. And I think, God, what a crummy day; I hate days like this. I blame it on the day.

But today I had a great experience in applying what we've learned here. When the children came in the door for lunch, the big one came falling in. He had been pushed by the younger one. Then they proceeded to fight all the way through lunch, kicking each other under the table and saying, "I hate you!" "You're such a dummy!" "You pig face!" I thought, God, I've been meditating and my day has been very peaceful, and here they go again. I suppose they're going to fight all day. Then I thought, I don't have to get into it. I had been starting to get angry, but then I just began to watch them. I thought, It'll just pass like everything else, and my anger just drifted away. I didn't express my initial anger, but at the same time, I didn't think to myself, You shouldn't be angry. I was just not in the mood to get all riled up. So I thought to myself, Oh, so you're angry, Sue. That's all right. And it just went away.

In the next meeting Sue told the group:

This week I tried to watch my thoughts and emotions. I'd notice a thought or subtle emotion and I'd describe it to myself and clarify what it was. I would say, Now see how you were angry right there. Did you notice how the anger was building up and how you can feel it going now?

One day we were sitting at the dinner table. My husband and son were planning to go to a baseball game. I said, "Maybe I'll go along, too." And my son replied, "Oh, I wanted to go just with Dad." The first thing I was going to say to him was, "Well, that's not a very nice thing to say!" It was just about to come out of my mouth. Then I wondered, Why do I think that's not a nice thing to say? That implies that the nice thing would be not saying how he feels. He would grow up thinking that when he has feelings like that, they're not nice. I was thinking about how much of that must be programmed into me and how that judgment must affect the way I look at everything. The judgments I make about my thoughts cause a lot of the conflict that goes on inside of me. It's not so much the thoughts themselves, but there's judgment that goes along with just about everything I think: It's not nice; It's not good; or, It's not healthy.

It was interesting to see those feelings come up inside myself. I also remember thinking, They'll go and have a good time and I'm going to be home bored. I was getting all involved in those thoughts, starting to feel real sorry for myself. It was strange to see how one thing can trigger so many thoughts and feelings.

Then I watched to see when the day came. They did indeed go off to the baseball game. I was remembering how I had projected that I would be real sad all by myself, but that didn't actually happen. That had only existed in thought, and yet while I was experiencing those thoughts, I started to feel down: "poor me." It was all because of what I was thinking. It didn't turn out that way at all. I see that the thoughts that come through my mind and the judgments that I make are what cause me trouble, not what's actually going on in life moment by moment.

These excerpts show that developing a neutral observing attitude can be valuable for dealing effectively with the practical matters of everyday life. The observing consciousness is able to see through the self-created fantasies, dramas, conflicts, and emotional reactions that occur day to day. It stands as a center of stability for the individual as he is tossed and turned by the tumultuous mind and external world. As one identifies ever more completely with the observing consciousness, he increasingly appreciates the order, lawfulness, and harmony that underlie the confusion and discord in the world of names and forms. At the ajna chakra, the world of polarities is all but transcended. The witnessing consciousness does not identify with the world of distinctions and polarities it observes. It remains aware of the multiplicity but does not react to it, for it is also aware of an underlying unity. It is a transitional state between the dualistic consciousness of the vishuddha chakra and the non-dual consciousness of the seventh chakra, sahasrara. At the ajna chakra, one witnesses the illusory forms, but at sahasrara, the insubstantiality of the forms becomes fully apparent.

## INTERACTION AMONG THE CHAKRAS

In observing another person, one can easily be misled as to which archetype is predominant. Certain behaviors or aspects of life may seem to represent a particular mode of experience, but the person involved in that activity may be experiencing something quite different. For example, if a couple is in a sexual embrace, it may appear that they are absorbed in experiencing sensory pleasure. But in actuality one of the pair may be preoccupied with dominating and controlling the other; he, for instance, may be using sexual activity to assert his ego or to prove that he is adequate. Or, alternatively, he may be absorbed in the experience of love or devotion for his partner, rather than focusing on sensory pleasure.

A religious institution, such as a church or synagogue, stands for or represents experiences of the heart and throat chakras. The stated purpose of such institutions is to help one transcend the ego by serving others and surrendering to God. But the actions carried out in the name of a church or synagogue may actually foster another mode of consciousness. For instance, a self-styled holy crusade may lead many people to become absorbed in the muladhara chakra. The following psychotherapy excerpt illustrates the way religion may foster muladhara consciousness in a child:

> I've been incapacitated by fear my whole life. Fear is still there, and it's done terrible things to me. I was especially unhappy during my grade school years. I was frightened and anxious. I was very afraid of going to hell. My religion concentrated on sin and evil and on the consequences of that, and there was a really heavy emphasis on that in my home. I was always afraid of doing the wrong thing and of going to hell, which was always described very vividly. I was taught that if you committed a mortal sin and you died, you would go straight to hell. Well, there were a couple of times when I was a kid that I thought I had committed a mortal sin, and let me tell you, I went through hell without even dying. I got so sick

I couldn't go to school. I was vomiting, and just from fear. When I think about it now, I just get so angry that...(crying) To do that to a little child...

A person may also distort spiritual practices on his own and use them to maintain a less evolved mode of consciousness. For example, as in the following instance, yoga practices may be subverted by the ego to reinforce one's egoistic orientation rather than being used to establish a higher mode of consciousness:

When I started yoga and meditation, I decided that I was on a spiritual quest. I began eating differently, being disciplined, getting up early and doing hatha yoga and meditation. I thought I was being spiritual, but I really wasn't. I would think, I'm a meditator; she's not a meditator. I don't eat meat; he does eat meat. It was a way of saying, I'm a little better. It was just the same old thing that I had done all my life: I went to college and you didn't; I don't drink and you do. Now I realize that spirituality is beyond such distinctions.

For simplicity's sake, the chakras have been described separately in this book, but that is not meant to imply that a particular experience necessarily represents only one mode of consciousness and no other. Most experiences consist of dramas being carried on at more than one level simultaneously or in rapid succession. For example, sexual teasing may involve both sensory pleasure and experiences related to dominance and submission; and while eating food, one may experience sensory gratification as well as nurturance.

The third and fifth chakras functioning together lead one to establish an ego ideal. In this mode of functioning, one projects ideal or archetypal qualities upon his own ego as he would like it to be. Such projection may lead one to feel buoyed up. It may, however, have the opposite effect, as the following client has discovered:

I get attached to an image of how I'd like to be. I can see that I'm attached to some ideal. I ask myself how I would appear to be if I were enlightened. I envision myself as being very soft-spoken and gentle, as having a sense of depth in my eyes, as being someone who is not affected by another person's anger, someone who can absorb negative things and can say something to help people, who is understanding and who radiates a sense of warmth. There is a real attachment to that image. I think, Why can't I be like that? I see myself falling short of that ideal, and so I get into a rut, putting myself down because I'm not there.

Examples have already been given of a more evolved chakra being used in the service of a less evolved mode of consciousness. For instance, it was noted that the objectivity, understanding, or psychic experiences attained through the ajna chakra may be usurped by the ego to demonstrate one's superiority. A less evolved mode of experience may also be used in the service of a more enlightened mode of consciousness. For example, one who has acquired wisdom and understanding through the ajna chakra may wish to build an organization in order to teach and guide others. To accomplish his goal he may use the egoistic mode of consciousness, but he will not regard the organization as a possession or remain identified with or judge his self-worth in terms of the organization's accomplishments.

## NON-DUAL CONSCIOUSNESS

At the seventh chakra, sahasrara, at the crown of the head, one experiences a state of pure consciousness, unencumbered by any instruments or limiting forms. The mind-created grid of time, space, and causation is transcended. All polarities are united and all forms dissolved. One awakens from the illusory world of distinctions and multiplicity. "Sahasrara ... is the center beyond duality."[8] Here one experiences "a union that is simultaneously the fulfillment and dissolution of the worlds of sound, form, and contemplation."[9] At sahasrara there are no longer any melodramas or scenarios; even the realm of archetypes is left behind. Having reached this center, there is nothing more to be attained, nothing more to be known. One knows himself as the All in all; he realizes himself as the atman (Self) or unitary consciousness.

Since reductive psychologies do not acknowledge the existence of the Self or pure consciousness, and dualistic psychologies do not recognize that one can attain consciousness of the Self, those psychologies offer no methods for reaching this mode of consciousness. Dualistic psychologies can at best offer means for attaining glimmerings of the Self through its symbolic expression. Archetypal psychologies have studied symbols of the Self as found in dreams, myths, and spiritual traditions. They are capable of helping clients to recognize what may be called messages from the Self that may guide the ego and lead one to experience greater harmony and integration, but they do not conceive of the possibility of directly experiencing the Self. By contrast, all the methods of yoga are meant to lead a person step by step to the realization of his true nature as pure consciousness. According to yoga psychology, the realms of consciousness experienced at lower chakras are all preparatory to self-realization. The first six chakras are the way stations on the road to realization of the Self, and the various practices of yoga are designed to facilitate the journey.

Yogic practices have traditionally been divided into distinct branches, each of which develops a particular mode of consciousness.[10] A person may follow one or more of these paths, according to the qualities that he wishes to cultivate within himself. In the practice of karma yoga, one learns how to perform actions in the service of others without concern for reward. Karma yoga leads one out of the primitive modes of consciousness to the experience characteristic of the anahata chakra. Bhakti yoga is the yoga of devotion. In this path, one chooses a particular ideal or divine form and develops an intimate relationship with that ideal through devotional practices. All of one's emotions are directed upward toward that divine form, and one's entire life becomes an expression of surrender to that ideal. The practice of bhakti yoga brings one's consciousness more fully into the vishuddha chakra. One then enjoys that free-flowing sustenance that has been referred to as divine nectar, ambrosia, manna, and the fountain of youth. Raja yoga is a more comprehensive, objective, and systematic approach to human evolution. It includes systematic practices that culminate in concentration, meditation, and *samadhi*. Through those practices, one becomes a neutral observer of the dramas of life. He eventually learns to stop identifying with the dramas and approaches awareness of himself as pure consciousness. He becomes absorbed in the ajna chakra.

Finally, the practices of jnana yoga and laya yoga lead one to the unitary consciousness of sahasrara. Laya yoga is the yoga of dissolution. In following this path, the student dissolves all identification with the world of names and forms so that the Self alone remains. Jnana yoga uses contemplation to help one realize that everything that exists in the world of form is insubstantial and illusory. Both laya yoga and jnana yoga use the method of negation, which involves the rejection or dissolution of all that is false until there is nothing more to be discarded. One need only let go of all limiting conceptions and identifications to realize his true nature as unitary consciousness.

There are many ways of following the path of negation. In one practice, the aspirant sits quietly and repeatedly asks himself the question, Who am I? When a response to the question arises in the mind, such as "I am a male," he does not accept that limited polarized identification. He lets go of that thought and asks again, Who am I? Each subsequent response is discarded, for every answer to the question implies limitation. One continues to ask and to reject all the definitions that he ordinarily applies to himself. This is not an intellectual process—one is not merely rejecting a thought about oneself for the moment. The aim of the process is to fully realize that one is not a male as distinct from a female, a good person as distinct from a bad, that he need not identify with any particular qualities and reject others. One may practice this method daily, often going over and rejecting answers similar to those given the day before. Very gradually, one comes to experience that he is not any limited quality he has attributed to himself. The limitations of self-imposed attributes begin to fall away from his thoughts, desires, and actions. The following client described her experience with this practice as it has been adapted in mime:

> When we start our performance, we go through a process very much like contemplation in yoga. I slowly walk up to the stage, and with the first step, I ask myself, Who am I? And I consider the first thing that comes to mind: "Janet, a married woman," and everything that means to me. I take a good look at it and then I try to move one step closer to who I *really* am, which is the universal Self. I leave that married Janet back there and again question, Who am I? and I deal with the next thing that comes and then take another step. I keep taking steps, trying to reach a more universal Self, and when I feel that I have reached as far as I can go for the day, I pause and just let the movement evolve from within myself.

If one follows this method within the yoga tradition, one may eventually be able to wholly cease identifying with all limiting attributes, achieving a breakthrough in which he truly recognizes that he is beyond any of the distinctions that make up the world of names and forms. There are in yoga various other methods of attaining this end, but they all involve a similar process of negation and dissolution. For instance, in the practice of meditation one learns to disentangle himself from identification with the thoughts that come before his mind. In more evolved stages of meditation, one may even give up his identification with the mantra or object of meditation in order to experience consciousness beyond form.

## Silence

The practice of meditation involves a temporary retreat from the world of activity in order that one may find a neutral center of observation within, a center unaffected by external events and by one's emotions and thoughts. The experience may be compared to sitting in the eye of a hurricane: all around, there is a frantic whirlwind of activity, but at the center all is calm and at peace. Here one may observe the restless activity without getting swept up into it.

The meditator sits without movement in a quiet place, his eyes closed. He withdraws his senses from the outer world and also withdraws from his identification with thoughts, emotions, and desires, to a neutral observing consciousness. This solitude and silence lead one to that which lies behind and beyond the activity of the body, emotions, mind, and external environment. In that stillness, one experiences a state of great peace and satisfaction.

The restriction of environmental stimulation has been an important part of traditional therapeutic practices throughout the ages. Both the ancient Greeks and the American Indians, among others, put disturbed members of their societies into environments in which they were isolated from external stimulation in order to heal them.

> The treatment of the mentally ill by the use of "darkness [which] quiets the spirit" was already ascribed to the ancients in a medical treatise written by a first-century Roman, Aulus Cornelius Celsus. It was still the practice in the Middle Ages, along with reduced social and sensory stimulation. As [a] review of the history of psychiatry makes clear, solitude, darkness, silence, immobilization, and other forms of restricted environmental stimulation techniques were frequently recommended and used during the Renaissance, the Enlightenment, the Industrial Revolution, and so on without interruption to today."[11]

The practice of solitude and silence is also an important aspect of yoga therapy and extends beyond the practice of meditation. Certain clients may be invited to spend from one to ten days in retreat. During that time, their duties and activities in the external world are suspended; external demands and disturbances are minimized. One need not even prepare his food; meals are provided for him. He is asked to refrain from contact with others—except for counseling sessions that may occur daily—and is dissuaded from filling his time by reading books. Instead, he is encouraged to be with himself.

In the absence of external stimuli, one's thoughts and desires take center stage. During the first days of solitude, one typically notices how restless the mind is and how intense and demanding are his thoughts and emotions. Many thoughts and desires that have been in the back of his mind now have the open space to come forward into the light of consciousness. These disturb him and lead him to become restless. However, as the days pass and one maintains an observing attitude rather than acting on his thoughts, fantasies, emotions, and desires, the disturbances become less intense, and gradually dissipate. One feels refreshed and renewed; he experiences an inner calm like that after a storm. His gait becomes more relaxed, his face loses wrinkles, its worried look is replaced by a soft radiance, and he appears younger. He becomes aware of and enjoys subtleties in his environment and in his inner states that he did not experience before. He finds himself becoming more playful and begins to laugh spontaneously and joyfully as he notices the humor in the dramas of life taking place around him.

This is an intense practice undertaken only by those who have prepared themselves. Most people are not ready to be with themselves without distractions. Some clients in yoga therapy would find this practice unsettling; it would be more appropriate for them to attend a short seminar in a retreat-like setting with limited periods of silence. The yoga therapist may also encourage some clients to practice silence periodically while remaining in their normal environments. The client may remain silent for an entire day while carrying on his normal routine, including interacting with others. This practice helps one refrain from reacting to internal and external stimuli and increases his skills in observing himself and others. When one has a desire to speak and refrains from speaking, he may realize that he wanted to speak in order to hide his feelings or boost his ego. He realizes how much energy is dissipated in chatter and becomes aware of the insecurity, defensiveness, and wish to control others that often prompt one to speak. Those who practice silence are often surprised at the joy and spontaneity that can arise as they relate to others without speech.

Occasionally, periods of silence occur during therapy sessions, but many clients feel that they must talk continuously in order to accomplish as much as possible in therapy. They believe that their time is wasted if there is silence. However, according to the monistic paradigm, being silent can be of much greater value than filling all the empty spaces with talk. It allows one to hear the subtle promptings of his deepest self. The following discussion occurred after a ten-minute silence at the beginning of a group therapy session:

C1: *I can't stand it! I have nothing to say. I just can't take sitting here in silence.*

C2: *This is the first time I've been able to sit without becoming uncomfortable. It's kind of nice just to be quiet. I thought of several things that I could talk about, but none of them really seemed that important, so it felt better just to be quiet.*

C1: *I can't stand it!*

T: *Is it just here that you're uncomfortable with silence? Do you feel that way at other times?*

C1: *I do find that if I have a telephone conversation, I can't tolerate it if there's a void. I have to fill it. I always think of something to say, meaningless or not. I feel compelled.*

(*Two-minute pause*)

C1: *Do you want me to talk about something important? I'll tell you about my illness. I have this pain in my back. (Client continues talking about her illness. Therapist stretches out across two chairs. He is about to doze off.)*

C2 (*to therapist*): *What are you doing? I've never seen you in a prone position.*

C1: *Is this too boring?*

T: *I lost interest when you stole our silence. I felt that you were sharing more in your silence and in telling us your feelings about the silence than in talking about your illness.*

C2: *Are you really comfortable inside when we all sit here silently?*

T: *I was today. I don't always feel comfortable in silence. I'm comfortable if I feel there's not an expectation. If I create an expectation, for example, that silence means the group's not performing as it should be or that I should be directing the group, then I get anxious. But if I can just be here and be open, then the silence feels good, and I become aware of a lot of sharing.*

C2: *There are times when I would like to be able to appreciate silence with others, but unless it's something that's agreed upon ahead of time, unless we've all sat down and said, "Let's all be quiet," it's awkward, even with my husband and children.*

C3: *I noticed that a program is offered here in which one spends five days in silence. Maybe my life would be simpler if I go through that program and become less cluttered with emotions.*

C4: *I went through that practice, and I learned that a lot of what I say is not very meaningful. I realized that I often finish other people's thoughts and sentences. If people can't think of a word, I'll be right there to take care of them.*

*I wasn't completely comfortable sitting here in silence. What I find most difficult is knowing where to look. It's difficult for me to look anyone in the eye. I'll look at someone and then I'll have to look away.*

T: *What makes it difficult?*

C4: *It's too intimate, looking directly into someone's eyes. I'm not used to that kind of intimacy. But one day, a very good friend and I went to the park for a couple of hours. I said, "Let's be silent," and it was wonderful.*

C2: *My mouth has to be flapping all the time, except when I'm alone. I've been wondering what it would be like to be a more quiet person. I wonder what you see when you're more quiet with people. I'm always filling in and jabbering and finishing people's sentences.*

T: *You could try keeping silence for a day.*

C2: *I tried one day at home. It was fun. We acted things out instead of talking.*

C4: *When I practiced silence for five days, I was more in touch with what was going on than I am when I'm talking. When I'm talking, I have a one-track mind. I'm not as aware and attentive to people, to the expressions on their faces or what they're doing or saying. When I'm talking, I'm just busy, and a lot of things are blocked out.*

C3: *I've noticed that the attitude toward silence seems to vary in different forms of therapy. In meditative therapy, the principle seems to be: Be still within yourself and let things rise up and let them go. In Western therapies, you just sit there and try and talk it out. I've gone through the talking-out bit. I'm not so sure it worked.*

Another client had been in psychotherapy for several months. He usually talked nonstop, describing his struggles to change his habitual patterns of living. He wanted to get in as much as possible in the limited time we had together. In the middle of one session, however, he stopped speaking. After some minutes of thoughtful silence, he said:

C: *This is the first time that I've been in therapy where I've been able to just stop talking for a period of time and not feel totally threatened. I feel that I should be talking when I'm here because it's through talking that I gain awareness. But I'm beginning to realize that through the talking, I protect myself from another type of awareness that might be too painful to deal with.*

*(Ten-minute pause)*

C: *I'm thinking that if I were quiet for periods of time, certain thoughts or feelings might come up that I feel are potentially threatening to me.*

*(Fifteen-minute pause)*

C: *The feeling I now have about being silent is that there is a certain amount of comfort, security, and love.*

T: *Just the opposite of what you were saying before—that in the silence, you felt insecurity.*

C: *I was afraid of the silence. Things would come up that I was afraid to deal with. But now I feel a sense of calm, not a lot of anxiety about being silent. I was thinking about what the womb would feel like, being enveloped by silence, very secure.*

*I never thought of therapy as being relaxing. I've had this preconditioned notion that it has to be high powered and tense. The last thing that I could ever imagine therapy being is relaxing. The structure here, I now realize, is very loose and flexible. It is what I bring to the structure that is limiting. To feel that relaxation and know that I won't be judged or feel embarrassed is really amazing. I was looking for some type of change with a preconceived notion about how I would go about changing, imposing an old structure on an unknown and hoping that something new would come of it.*

*Because I was able to stop today and just be quiet, I feel I've discovered that new dimension that I was looking for so desperately. It's obvious in a way, and yet what has been most obvious, I have often overlooked.*

*(Five-minute pause)*

C: *What do you feel when I'm not saying anything?*

T: *I feel more in contact than in any other meeting we've had.*

C: *I realize that in our sessions, I've been beating myself to death. Now I know that I don't have to do that. It has been a refreshing and delightful experience. I expected something terrible to come out of the silence, but I feel good. I feel joy.*

Silence and solitude are means of separating oneself from the melodramas of the world. One's inner turmoil then comes to the foreground of consciousness. One must remain still, observing the play of the personal unconscious and the collective unconscious; he must learn detachment from both their alluring and their demonic forms and plots. If one maintains his stillness and silence, he will pass beyond the restless, turbulent, ever-changing forms of the phenomenal world and enter a quiet haven of pure formless being. This state of consciousness is the ground of all being, for all forms arise out of it.

Progressing through each of the first five chakras, one experiences a new and more subtle variation of the game of hide-and-seek. In each of those chakras, there is a subject that seeks after an object or state that is distinct from it. One may seek security, pleasure, status, the object of his devotion, or countless other goals. At the sixth chakra, the ajna chakra, one recognizes the game for what it is, and at sahasrara, the seventh chakra, the game is over; one is no longer playing hide-and-seek, for one is found. He has found himself. He realizes that he has been both the seeker and the alluring goal. The years and millennia spent in separation, darkness, delusion, disappointment, in happiness and sorrow, pleasure and grief, are over. One who has so often been weary finally awakens refreshed to find that the entire extravaganza, with all its uncountable forms, plots, attainments, victories, defeats, discoveries, losses, loves, hates, deaths, and births, was all a dream. One's destiny is to realize his true nature as that illimitable, immortal consciousness that is *sat-chit-ananda*— existence, knowledge, and bliss. The Upanishads echo through the ages: "*Tat tvam asi*, 'Thou art That.' Awaken from this dream and realize your true Self."

# REFERENCES AND NOTES

CW = *The Collected Works of C. G. Jung*. Edited by Herbert Read, Michael Fordham, and Gerhard Adler. Translated by R. F. C. Hull. Bollingen Series, no. 20. 18 volumes. Princeton, N.J.: Princeton University Press; London: Routledge & Kegan Paul, 1953–80. All references are to volume and paragraph, and are reprinted with permission of the publishers.

*Chapter 1*
THE ECOLOGY OF CONSCIOUSNESS

1. Richard H. Svihus, M.D., "The Dimensions of Wellness: The Holistic Viewpont," *American Holistic Medicine* 1, no. 1 (February 1979): 19.
2. Ibid. Quoted from the Apostle Paul in 1 Thess. 5:23.

*Chapter 2*
BODY AND BEHAVIORAL TECHNIQUES

1. The book *Diet and Nutrition: A Holistic Approach* by Rudolph Ballentine, M.D. (Honesdale, Pa.: Himalayan Institute Press, 1978), discusses this aspect of yoga therapy in depth and is recommended for all those who wish further knowledge of the relation between food and consciousness.
2. W. Edward Mann, *Orgone, Reich and Eros: Wilhelm Reich's Theory of Life Energy* (New York: Simon and Schuster, Touchstone Books, 1973), 62.
3. Swami Vivekananda, *Raja-Yoga*, rev. ed. (New York: Ramakrishna-Vivekananda Center, 1955), 29.
4. Alexander Lowen, *Pleasure: A Creative Approach to Life* (New York: Penguin Books, 1975), 39–40.
5. Magda Proskauer, "Breathing Therapy," in *Ways of Growth*, ed. H. Otto and J. Mann (New York: Viking Press, 1968), 26.
6. Lowen, *Pleasure*, 38.
7. Ibid., 40.

8. See L. C. Lum, "The Syndrome of Habitual Chronic Hyperventilation," *Modern Trends in Psychosomatic Medicine* 13 (1976): 196–230.
9. Ibid., 226–27.
10. The therapeutic use of breathing techniques has been discussed further in Swami Rama, Rudolph Ballentine, M.D., and Alan Hymes, M.D., *Science of Breath: A Practical Guide* (Honesdale, Pa.: Himalayan Institute Press, 1979) and in ch. 6 of Phil Nuernberger, *Freedom from Stress: A Holistic Approach* (Honesdale, Pa.: Himalayan Institute Press, 1981).
11. *The Bhagavad Gita,* trans. Juan Mascaró (Hammondsworth, England: Penguin Books, 1962), 2:47, 2:49.
12. CW 11, 522.
13. These ten principles are discussed further in ch. 2 of Swami Rama, *Lectures on Yoga* (Honesdale, Pa.: Himalayan Institute Press, 1979).
14. Hellmuth Kaiser, *Effective Psychotherapy* (New York: Free Press, 1965), 36.
15. Virginia Satir, *Peoplemaking* (Palo Alto, Calif.: Science and Behavior Books, 1972), 60.
16. Ibid., 73–74.
17. Palo Alto, Calif.: Science and Behavior Books, 1975.

Chapter 3
THE RELATIONSHIP BETWEEN THERAPIST AND CLIENT

1. See, for example, Thomas S. Szasz, *The Myth of Mental Illness* (New York: Dell Publishing Co., Delta Books, 1961).
2. See, for example, Swami Rama, *A Practical Guide to Holistic Health* (Honesdale, Pa.: Himalayan Institute Press, 1980) and *Lectures on Yoga* (Honesdale, Pa.: Himalayan Institute Press, 1979).
3. Hellmuth Kaiser, *Effective Psychotherapy* (New York: Free Press, 1965), 3–4.
4. CW 16: 168, 170.
5. *The Bhagavad Gita,* trans. Juan Mascaró (Hammondsworth, England: Penguin Books, 1962), 3:21–24.
6. Lawrence M. Brammer and Everett L. Shostrom, *Ther-*

*apeutic Psychology: Fundamentals of Counseling and Psychotherapy* (Englewood Cliffs, N.J.: Prentice-Hall, 1960), 230.

7.  Judah C. Safier, "Hasidism, Faith, and the Therapeutic Paradox," in *Mystics and Medics: A Comparison of Mystical and Psychotherapeutic Encounters,* ed. Reuven P. Bulka (New York: Human Sciences Press, 1979), 57.

8.  Elie Wiesel, *Souls on Fire: Portraits and Legends of Hasidic Masters,* trans. Marion Wiesel (New York: Random House, Vintage Books, 1973), 51.

9.  Safier, "Hasidism, Faith, and the Therapeutic Paradox," 58.

10. Paul Watzlawick, The Language of Change: Elements of Therapeutic Communication (New York: Basic Books, 1978), 96.

*Chapter 4*
THE COLLECTIVE UNCONSCIOUS FROM THE YOGIC PERSPECTIVE

1.  Additional material on the relation between the chakras and one's functioning may be found in ch. 7 of Swami Rama, Rudolph Ballentine, M.D., and Swami Ajaya, *Yoga and Psychotherapy: The Evolution of Consciousness* (Honesdale, Pa.: Himalayan Institute Press, 1976).

2.  C. G. Jung, "Psychological Commentary on Kundalini Yoga, Lecture IV," *Spring: An Annual of Archetypal Psychology and Jungian Thought* 1976: 21, 27.

3.  CW 9, part 1, 467 n. 12.

4.  Jung, "Psychological Commentary on Kundalini Yoga, Lecture II," *Spring* 1975: 23.

5.  Jung, "Psychological Commentary on Kundalini Yoga, Lecture I," *Spring* 1975: 8.

6.  Jung, "Kundalini Yoga, Lecture II," 19–20.

7.  Violet S. de Laszlow, Introduction to C. G. Jung, *Psyche and Symbol* (Garden City, N.Y.: Doubleday and Co., Anchor Books, 1958), xxxi.

8.  C. G. Jung, *Memories, Dreams, Reflections* (New York: Random House, Vintage Books, 1963), 208–9.

9.  de Laszlow, Introduction to *Psyche and Symbol,* xxx–xxxi.

10. Jung, "Psychological Commentary on Kundalini Yoga, Lecture III," *Spring* 1976: 27–28.
11. Gerald R. Weeks and Luciano L'Abate, *Paradoxical Psychotherapy: Theory and Practice with Individuals, Couples, and Families* (New York: Brunner/Mazel, 1982), 19.
12. Jung, "Kundalini Yoga, Lecture II," 22.
13. See Swami Rama, *Enlightenment Without God: Mandukya Upanishad* (Honesdale, Pa.: Himalayan Institute Press, 1982), 55–65.
14. *The Bhagavad Gita*, trans. Juan Mascaró (Hammondsworth, England: Penguin Books, 1962), 2:62–66.
15. Jolande Jacobi, *The Psychology of C. G. Jung* (New Haven, Conn.: Yale University Press, 1973), 47n.
16. Alexander Lowen, *Pleasure: A Creative Approach to Life* (New York: Penguin Books, 1975), 15.
17. Erich Fromm, *To Have or to Be?* ed. Ruth Nanda Anshen (New York: Harper and Row, 1976), 170–71.
18. Bob Dylan, "Gotta Serve Somebody," *Slow Train Coming*, Columbia FCT 36120.
19. For an extensive discussion of karma yoga, see ch. 4 of Swami Rama, *Choosing a Path* (Honesdale, Pa.: Himalayan Institute Press, 1982).
20. *Bhagavad Gita*, trans. Mascaró, 2:48; 3:25.

Chapter 5
SPIRITUAL ASPECTS OF PSYCHOTHERAPY

1. Jung, "Psychological Commentary on Kundalini Yoga, Lecture III," *Spring: An Annual of Archetypal Psychology and Jungian Thought* 1976: 6.
2. Jung, "Psychological Commentary on Kundalini Yoga, Lecture II," *Spring* 1975: 22.
3. Psalm 23.
4. CW 11, 854.
5. CW 13, 36.
6. Jolande Jacobi, *The Psychology of C. G. Jung* (New Haven, Conn.: Yale University Press, 1973), 139.
7. Jung, "Psychological Commentary on Kundalini Yoga, Lecture IV," *Spring* 1976: 28.

8. Heinrich Zimmer, "The Chakras of Kundalini Yoga," *Spring* 1975: 34.
9. Ibid.
10. For a presentation of the major divisions of yogic practice, see *Choosing a Path* by Sri Swami Rama (Honesdale, Pa.: Himalayan Institute Press, 1982).
11. Peter Suedfeld, *Restricted Environmental Stimulation: Research and Clinical Applications* (New York: John Wiley and Sons, 1980), 218.

# ABOUT THE AUTHOR

 **Swami Ajaya, PhD,** received his education at Wesleyan University and at the University of California, Berkeley. He taught at the University of Wisconsin Medical School in Madison, Wisconsin, and served there as a consulting psychologist. In addition to his Western training, Swami Ajaya studied with various yogis in India. He is the author and co-author of numerous books, including *Yoga Psychology: A Practical Guide to Meditation* and *Yoga & Psychotherapy.*

# The Himalayan Institute

*The main building of the Institute headquarters near Honesdale, Pennsylvania*

FOUNDED IN 1971 BY SWAMI RAMA, the Himalayan Institute has been dedicated to helping people grow physically, mentally, and spiritually by combining the best knowledge of both the East and the West.

Our international headquarters is located on a beautiful 400-acre campus in the rolling hills of the Pocono Mountains of northeastern Pennsylvania. The atmosphere here is one to foster growth, increase inner awareness, and promote calm. Our grounds provide a wonderfully peaceful and healthy setting for our seminars and extended programs. Students from all over the world join us here to attend programs in such diverse areas as hatha yoga, meditation, stress reduction, ayurveda, nutrition, Eastern philosophy, psychology, and other subjects. Whether the programs are for weekend meditation retreats, week-long seminars on spirituality, month-long residential programs, or holistic health services, the attempt here is to provide an environment of gentle inner progress. We invite you to join with us in the ongoing process of personal growth and development.

The Institute is a nonprofit organization. Your membership in the Institute helps to support its programs. Please call or write for information on becoming a member.

## Programs and Services include:

- ▓ Weekend or extended seminars and workshops
- ▓ Meditation retreats and advanced
     meditation instruction
- ▓ Hatha yoga teachers training
- ▓ Residential programs for self-development
- ▓ Holistic health services and pancha karma at the
     Institute's Center for Health and Healing
- ▓ Spiritual excursions
- ▓ Varcho Veda® herbal products
- ▓ Himalayan Institute Press
- ▓ *Yoga + Joyful Living* magazine
- ▓ Sanskrit Home Study Course

A guide to programs and other offerings is free within the USA. To request a copy, or for further information, call 800-822-4547 or 570-253-5551; write to the Himalayan Institute, 952 Bethany Turnpike, Honesdale, PA 18431, USA; or visit our website at www.HimalayanInstitute.org.

# HIMALAYAN INSTITUTE® PRESS

THE HIMALAYAN INSTITUTE PRESS has long been regarded as the resource for holistic living. We publish dozens of titles, as well as audio and video tapes, that offer practical methods for living harmoniously and achieving inner balance. Our approach addresses the whole person—body, mind and spirit—integrating the latest scientific knowledge with ancient healing and self-development techniques.

As such, we offer a wide array of titles on physical and psychological health and well-being, spiritual growth through meditation and other yogic practices, as well as translations of yogic scriptures.

Our yoga accessories include the *Chakras:Purifying the Subtle Body* packet for meditation practice and the Neti Pot™, the ideal tool for sinus and allergy sufferers. The Varcho Veda® line of quality herbal extracts is now available to enhance balanced health and well-being.

Subscriptions are available to a bimonthly magazine, *Yoga + Joyful Living*, which offers thought-provoking articles on all aspects of meditation and yoga, including yoga's sister science, ayurveda.

For a free catalog call: 800-822-4547 or 570-253-5551
email: hibooks@HimalayanInstitute.org
fax: 570-647-6360
write: Himalayan Institute Press
   952 Bethany Tpke
   Honesdale PA 18431-1843

or visit our website at www.HimalayanInstitute.org

# enhance your practice

*Refine and deepen your meditation and asana with these valuable tools for practice.*

### Advanced Yoga Relaxations
### As Taught by the Himalayan Institute
*Rolf Sovik, PsyD*

Take your practice to the next level with three advanced techniques designed to help you learn to relax and meditate. 31 Points Exercise, 61 Points Exercise *(Shavayatra)*, and 75 Breaths Exercise *(Shitili Karana)* help to make the mind more focused and one-pointed.
CD270HWP / CD / 69:01 minutes / $18.95

### Guided Yoga Relaxations
*Rolf Sovik, PsyD*

Four relaxation and breathing methods help to soothe anxiety, improve sleep, and reduce stressful thoughts and emotions. In less than 15 minutes you'll feel rested, renewed, and on your way to a brighter day. These methods provide the foundation for more advanced practices.
CD238HWP / CD / 61:15 minutes / $18.95

### Yoga: Mastering the Basics

One convenient DVD provides progressive practice at beginner and intermediate levels. Two guided yoga routines by the authors of the award-winning book *Yoga: Mastering the Basics* include an introduction and clear, concise instruction by Sandra Anderson.

### Flexibility, Strength & Balance (45 minute routine)

A revitalizing gentle practice for all levels of experience to tone the body. Includes: Crocodile Pose *(Makarasana)*, Cat Pose, Cobra *(Bhujangasana)*, Reclining Twist, Guided Relaxation, and more.

**Deepen & Strengthen** (Intermediate, 60 minute routine)

Classic yoga postures incorporate breath awareness and more challenging postures. Requires strength and flexibility to train the muscles and joints. Includes: Sun Salutation *(Surya Namaskara)*, Triangle Pose *(Trikonasana)*, Locust Pose *(Shalabhasana)*, Inverted Action Pose *(Viparita Karani)*, Guided Relaxation and more.
VDVD0001MI / DVD Video (NTSC) / approx. 111 minutes / $24.95

HIMALAYAN
INSTITUTE®
PRESS

*for* ORDERS OR A FREE CATALOG OF BOOKS AND TOOLS FOR YOGA, MEDITATION, AND HEALTH
Call: 800-822-4547 or 570-253-5551 • Visit: www.HimalayanInstitute.org
Email: mailorder@HimalayanInstitute.org
Write: Himalayan Institute Press, 952 Bethany Turnpike, Honesdale, PA 18431

080405

# open your mind

## Moving Inward
The Journey to Meditation
*Rolf Sovik, Psy.D.*

Illustrated instructions and guidelines show readers of all levels how to transition from asanas to meditation. This book combines practical advice on breathing and relaxation with timeless asana postures.

*Moving Inward is a clear, seamless entry into the eight classical limbs of yoga . . . Highly recommended for students and teachers alike.*

—Lilias Folan,
*author of Lilias! Yoga Gets Better With Age*

Paperback with flaps / 204 pages / 6 x 9 / $14.95
ISBN 978-0-89389-247-5

## Meditation and Its Practice
*Swami Rama*

In clear, concise, easy-to-follow terms, this book provides all the basic tools for starting a meditation practice or deepening an existing one. Systematic and careful instruction covers all the basics of sitting postures, breathing and relaxation and using a mantra.

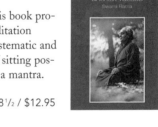

Paperback with flaps / 110 pages / 5$\frac{1}{2}$ x 8$\frac{1}{2}$ / $12.95
ISBN 978-0-89389-153-4

HIMALAYAN
INSTITUTE®
PRESS

070102b